THE BATTLE OF ARGINUSAE

WITNESS TO ANCIENT HISTORY

Greg Aldrete, *Series Editor*

Also in the Series:

Jerry Toner, *The Day Commodus Killed a Rhino: Understanding the Roman Games*

THE BATTLE OF ARGINUSAE

Victory at Sea and Its Tragic Aftermath in the Final Years of the Peloponnesian War

Debra Hamel

Johns Hopkins University Press
Baltimore

Printed in the United States of America on acid-free paper
2 4 6 8 9 7 5 3 1

Johns Hopkins University Press
2715 North Charles Street
Baltimore, Maryland 21218-4363
www.press.jhu.edu

Library of Congress Cataloging-in-Publication Data

Hamel, Debra.
The Battle of Arginusae : victory at sea and its tragic aftermath in the final years of the Peloponnesian War / Debra Hamel.
pages cm. — (Witness to ancient history)
Includes bibliographical references and index.
ISBN 978-1-4214-1680-9 (hardcover : alk. paper) — ISBN 978-1-4214-1681-6 (pbk. : alk. paper) — ISBN 978-1-4214-1682-3 (electronic) — ISBN 1-4214-1680-8 (hardcover : alk. paper) — ISBN 1-4214-1681-6 (pbk. : alk. paper) — ISBN 1-4214-1682-4 (electronic) 1. Arginusae, Battle of, Greece, 406 B.C. I. Title.
DF229.83.H36 2015
938'.05—dc23

2014030728

A catalog record for this book is available from the British Library.

Cartography by Bill Nelson.

For Clare, ἔφορος τῶν φερεοίκων

CONTENTS

ACKNOWLEDGMENTS

My thanks to the usual suspects, Kyle Behen and Victor Bers, for their support, encouragement, and intellectual input lo these many years. Thanks also to Andrew Ruddle of the Trireme Trust and to Bill Nelson for his cartography. Matthew McAdam of Johns Hopkins University Press and series editor Greg Aldrete provided much useful feedback and made this a far more readable text than it would have been otherwise. Barbara Lamb, finally, saved me from countless errors with her meticulous copyediting. This book is dedicated to Clare Dudman, author and snail aficionado, with my thanks for her generous help, enthusiasm, and most of all, friendship.

TIMELINE

In some cases dates appear below with a slash, for example, 446/5. This is because the Athenian year ran from midsummer to midsummer. All dates listed are B.C. See also the appendixes for discussion of the timing of events in 406.

510	Hippias expelled from Athens
508/7	Cleisthenes' reforms
499	Athenians participate in Ionian Revolt
490	First Persian War (Battle of Marathon)
486	Xerxes succeeds Darius
483	Surplus revenue from Athenian silver mines
480–479	Second Persian War
480	Battles of Thermopylae, Artemisium, and Salamis
479	Battles of Plataea and Mycale; siege of Sestus
478	Formation of Delian League
c. 460–446/5	First Peloponnesian War
451 or 450	Greek and Persian hostilities cease
446/5	Thirty Years' Peace
431–404	Second Peloponnesian War
431–421	Archidamian, or Ten Years' War
431–425	Five Spartan invasions of Attica
430	Plague first hits Athens
428–427	Revolt of Mytilene
425	Athenians fortify Pylos
421–413	Peace of Nicias
418	Battle of Mantinea
415–413	Sicilian Expedition
413	Fortification of Decelea
413–404	Ionian War

411	Oligarchic revolution in Athens
411	Battles of Cynossema and Abydus
410	Battle of Cyzicus
407	Battle of Notium
406	Battle of Arginusae
405	Battle of Aegospotami
404	Surrender of Athens

MAPS

N
Strymon River
Amphipolis
MACEDON
Potidaea
Mount Athos
Corcyra
Sybota
Artemisium
Thermopylae
ACARNANIA
AETOLIA
Naupactus
Corinthian Gulf
BOEOTIA
Delium
Athens
ATTICA
PELOPONNESE
Corinth
Isthmus of Corinth
Mantinea
Eurotas River
Sparta
Pylos
Sphacteria
Cape Malea
0 10 20 30 40 50 mi
0 20 40 60 80 km

Map 1. Greece

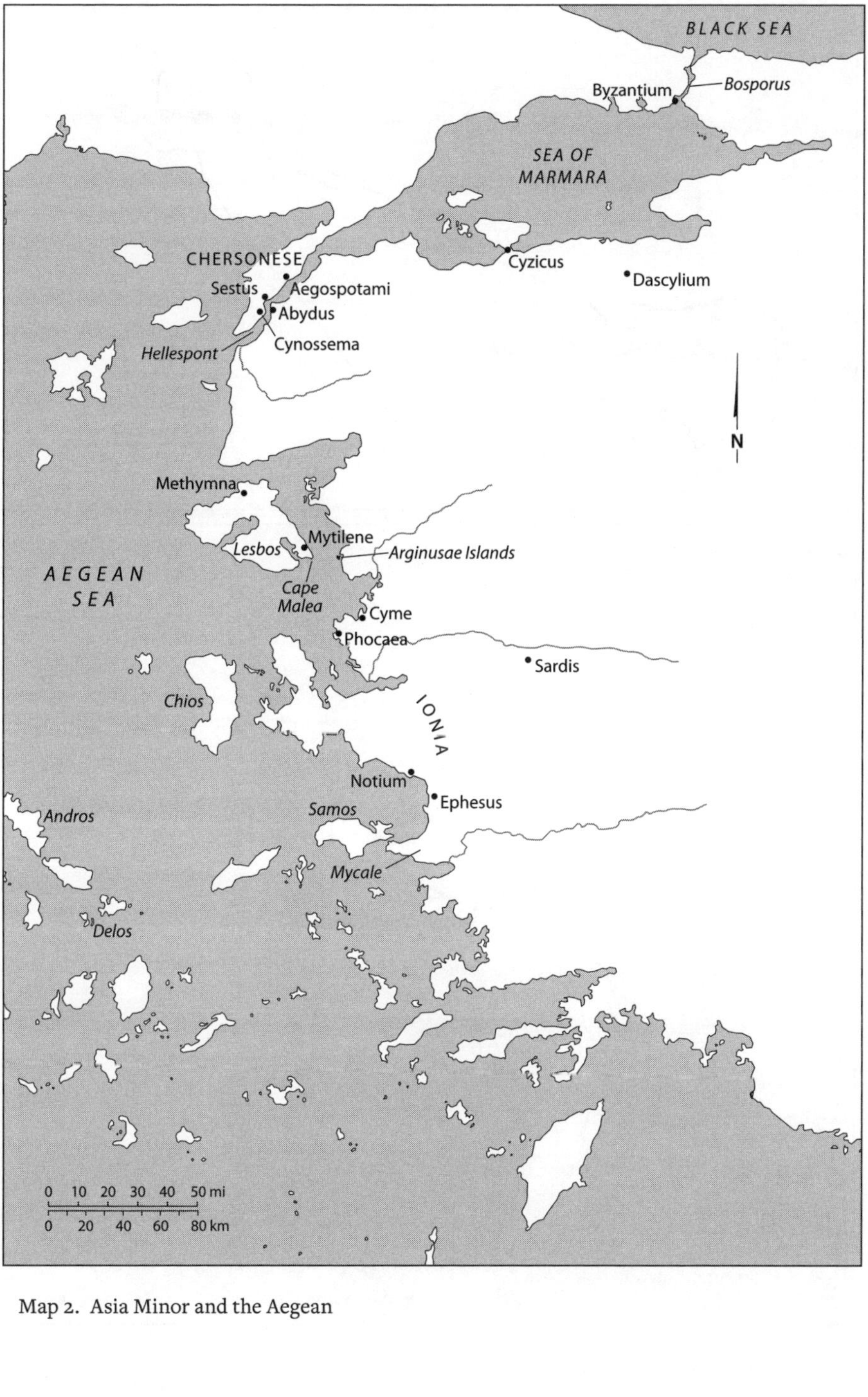

Map 2. Asia Minor and the Aegean

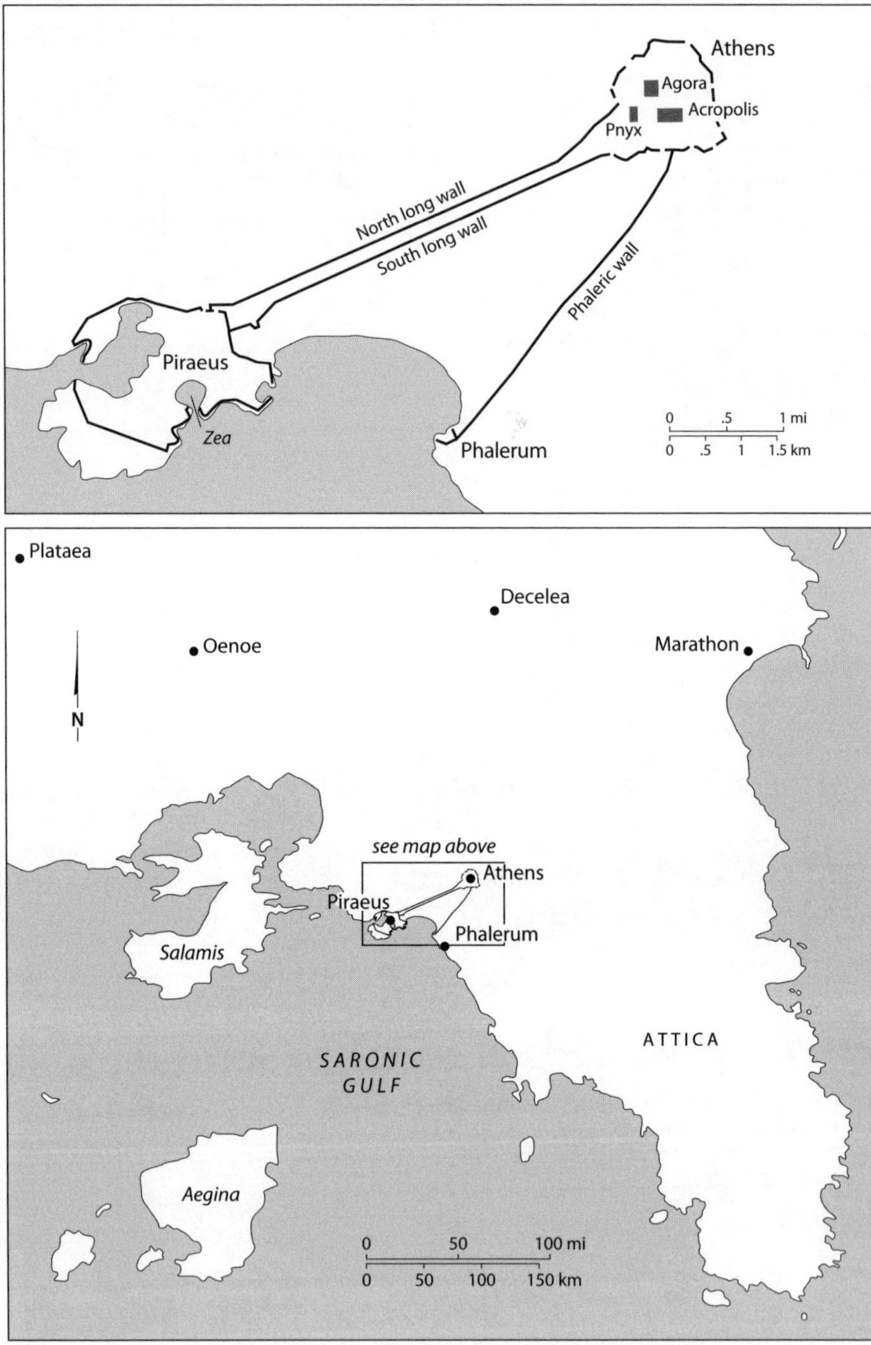

Map 3. Attica and the Saronic Gulf

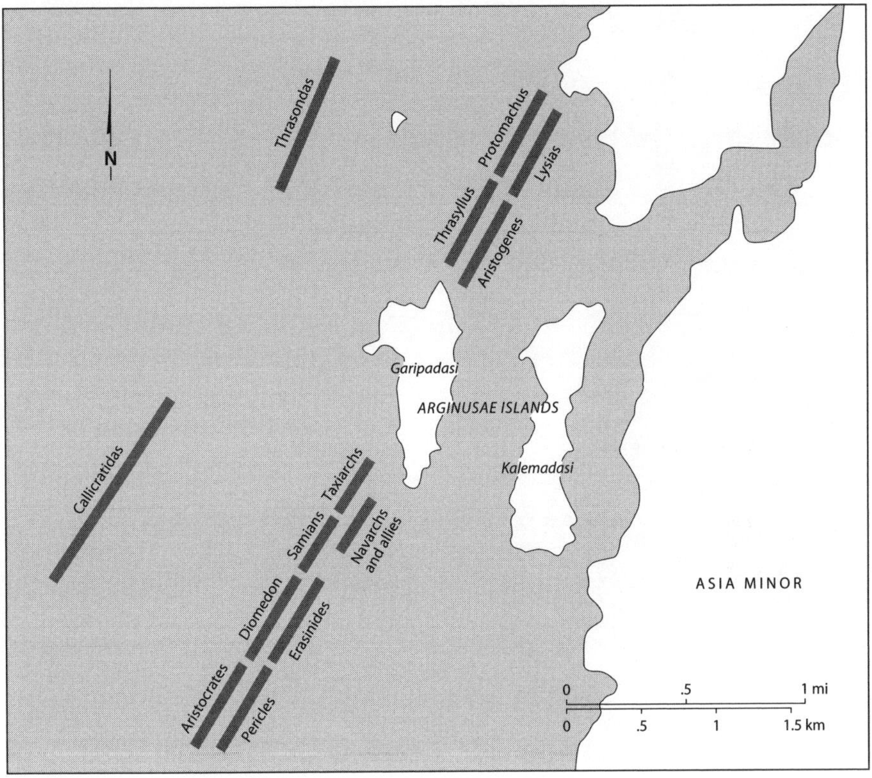

Map 4. The Battle of Arginusae

THE BATTLE OF ARGINUSAE

Prologue

IF YOU WERE TO FALL off a cruise ship into seventy-two degree water, you'd have a reasonable chance of surviving until help arrived, assuming you could stay afloat; water that temperature is unlikely to kill you for at least several hours. All bets are off, of course, if you also happen to be seriously injured—bleeding out after being stabbed in the gut with a sword, for example—which would severely diminish your expected survival time. On the particular summer day with which we'll be concerned in this book, in late July or early August of 406 B.C., there were many thousands of men in just this predicament, bobbing in the cool but not immediately deadly waters of the North Aegean, awaiting rescue—albeit not after a recreational cruise. Most of them were Spartans, or allies of Sparta, but our story has to do with the smaller contingent of Athenian bodies that were in the water. At the moment these men were sailors—oarsmen, most of them, with new blisters on their hands and buttocks that were now stinging in the salt water—but back in Athens just a few weeks earlier they'd been storekeepers or carpenters or farmers or slaves. Many of them had never served with Athens' fleet before, but they'd been called up for service in an emergency. Having done their duty for family and fatherland, they clung now to the wreckage of their wooden ships, their fingers becoming increasingly clumsy the colder they got, and they waited for the rescue boats to pick them up.[1]

The Athenians in the water had just taken part in an important naval battle, and their side had won the day, though they may not have known it. In a fight involving hundreds of ships stretched across miles of sea, it's impossible for any one person at water level to know much about the big picture. But even if they knew nothing for sure, they had reason to be hopeful. They weren't being picked off by enemy archers, and the Spartans weren't sailing among them and clubbing them with oar blades or spearing them like fish as they bobbed helplessly in the water. The injured might not make it, those who had been hit by enemy archers or who'd caught a Spartan's sword or spear when the ships were close enough for the enemy to board. Or maybe they had been hurt on impact, slammed against the ribs of their vessel when a Spartan warship rammed it, opening a hole in the hull. But the rest of them had a fighting chance, if only they could hold out long enough for help to arrive.

We'll find out what happened to these thousand or more shipwrecked Athenians later in this book. For now we'll leave them clinging to the fractured hulls of their vessels while we consider how they came to be there. The short answer to that question is that their vessels had been damaged in a battle at sea off the coast of Asia Minor (modern Turkey) east of Lesbos and west of the Arginusae Islands, from which the battle took its name. The Battle of Arginusae was fought between the Athenians and the Spartans late in the Peloponnesian War, which was now in its twenty-sixth year. A generation had grown up in Athens since a Spartan army kicked off the war by invading Athenian territory in the spring of 431. The Spartans had been unable to inflict much real damage as long as they confined themselves to attacks on Athens' homeland, but the long war brought changes. The famously conservative Spartans, who had long fielded the most fearsome infantry in ancient Greece, had ultimately adapted their strategy to the needs of the moment and gone to sea, putting into motion a strategy aimed at undermining Athens' naval empire. The summer of 406 found them in the North Aegean attacking an ally of Athens on the island of Lesbos. More than a month later that attack resulted in a showdown with the Athenians themselves, whose 150 warships had taken up position off the tiny Arginusae islands.

The Battle of Arginusae was the largest naval battle that had ever been fought between Greeks, with nearly three hundred ships involved in the fight.[2] It also turned out to be the Athenians' last victory of the war. The win was not a foregone conclusion, as the Spartan fleet they fought was more experienced. This in itself is noteworthy, since Athens historically had by far the better navy. But the Athenians had had to respond to a crisis by hastily putting a fleet together, and they had pretty much scraped the bottom of the barrel in manning it. Everything depended on the ships they had in the water at Arginusae. Losing the battle would almost certainly have meant their total defeat in the war—and defeat, in the ancient world, very often meant the annihilation of one's population, fathers and brothers and sons executed to a man, the women and children sold into slavery. Athens' victory, then, hardly to be hoped for, was cause for relief and joy and celebration back in Athens. Paradoxically, Arginusae was also one of the worst disasters that befell the Athenians in the twenty-seven years of their war with Sparta.

This book tells the story of the Battle of Arginusae and its horrible aftermath, what happened on the water and back in Athens that turned the victory into one of the most infamous chapters in the city-state's history. The book begins by introducing readers to the two great superpowers of the fifth century B.C., Athens and Sparta, which had fought as allies in the early years of the century but came to be pitted against each other in its last decades. The first chapter also provides a summary of fifth-century history from the Second Persian War to the summer of 406, when the Athenians launched the fleet, manned by inexperienced crews, that would fight at Arginusae. Chapter 2, the first of two thematic chapters in the book, discusses Greek naval warfare—the ships and tactics that had put the Persians to rout at the Battle of Salamis in 479 and had since earned Athens her naval empire. We return to the historical narrative in chapter 3, which discusses Arginusae itself, from the Athenians' preparation of their fleet to the battle and its immediate aftermath. This is where readers will find out what happened to the shipwrecked sailors who were awaiting rescue after Athens' victory. Chapter 4 concerns the relationship between the Athenians' democratic government and their generals. The discussion prepares for the subject of chapter 5, what happened back in Athens when news of the fleet's victory and its consequences became known to the Athenians. The book closes with a brief look at the end of the Peloponnesian War and at the damage the Arginusae affair has done to Athens' reputation in the millennia since the battle was fought.

-1-

Setting the Stage: From Xerxes' Invasion to the Eve of Arginusae

Athens was supreme and almost as untouchable by sea as the Spartans were on land. The irresistible force could not meet the immovable object.

George Cawkwell, *Thucydides and the Peloponnesian War*

SOON AFTER XERXES, the king of Persia, crossed into Europe in 480 B.C. on his way to conquer Greece, his men saw something that should have given him pause: a horse gave birth to a hare—or so Herodotus tells us in his *History of the Persian Wars*. The meaning of the portent was clear enough as far as Herodotus was concerned: the Persians would enter Greece in splendor, but they'd be running like rabbits on the way out.[1] And so it went. The Persians marched west across southern Europe and south through Greece. They managed, despite suffering great losses, to muscle their way through a pass at Thermopylae in central Greece, leaving King Leonidas and his three hundred Spartans dead in their wake. At the same time the Persian fleet fought a series of inconclusive naval battles against the Greeks. But when Thermopylae fell, the Greeks fell back. They wound up stationed at Salamis, an island not quite a mile off the west coast of Attica. The ensuing battle in the narrow strait between Salamis and the mainland was a devastating loss for the Persians. They had yet to lose the war: they would do that in a pair of land battles the following year. But the loss at Salamis changed everything. It prompted Xerxes to return to Persia with what was left of his fleet, his men running like rabbits, or at least rowing like rabbits, in their haste to get out of Greek waters.

Back before things started going badly for Xerxes, no one would have bet his pension on a Greek victory over Persia. Persia was a vast empire that stretched from Egypt to the Indus River, encompassing more land than the Roman Empire would at its height.[2] It had been an expansionist power for some seventy years, swallowing up whole nations, rolling west across Asia and into North Africa. Most recently the Persians had cut a swath across the north Aegean to Macedon. Greece, which lay just to the south of Macedon, was simply next in line to be absorbed. By comparison with the Persian behemoth, Greece was tiny, with correspondingly fewer resources: Xerxes almost certainly brought with him to Greece far more men and ships than his enemy could muster.

Greece was not only dwarfed by its adversary, it was also at a disadvantage because it was not a united nation. It was composed of hundreds of small, independent city-states, or *poleis*, which were very often at war with one another. The Greeks shared a common culture. They worshipped the same gods and spoke mutually intelligible dialects of the same language. They recognized a shared Greekness. But that didn't stop them from regularly killing one another in battle. When the Greeks faced an existential threat from Persia, however, many of them (not all: some poleis wound up siding with Persia) put aside their private disputes and formed a league to combat their common enemy—what modern scholars call the Hellenic League. Two poleis in particular played a crucial role in the fight against Persia. One was widely recognized as preeminent among the Greeks in infantry battle. The other contributed the largest number of ships to the allied Greek fleet.

Sparta

The first of these two dominant poleis was Sparta, whose capital lay some twenty-five miles inland on the banks of the Eurotas River in the Peloponnese. In the eighth century B.C., when many other city-states began siphoning off their surplus populations by establishing colonies throughout the Mediterranean, Sparta opted to meet its need for more land by subjugating and enslaving its neighbors to the south and west. Later the Spartans further expanded their influence through a series of individual alliances with other states, most but not all of them in the Peloponnese. Sparta was the hegemonic power in this complex of inter-polis ties, which historians call the Peloponnesian League. By the time Xerxes invaded Greece in 480, then, Sparta directly controlled or was allied with nearly all the city-states in the Peloponnese.

Some of the Peloponnesians whom the Spartans subjugated wound up as *perioikoi*—literally, “dwellers around”—residents of Spartan territory who were free but lacked full citizenship rights. The far less fortunate victims of Spartan expansion, however, were the helots, or “captured ones,” whom historian Paul Cartledge rightly calls “the single most important human fact about ancient Sparta.” The helots were kept as a state-owned servile class, many of them working as serflike farmers, tied to the land and required to surrender some portion of their produce to their masters; others served as personal slaves. They were brutally repressed—regularly beaten, killed with impunity. Indeed, you might say it was state policy to murder them on a regular basis. The ephors—elected Spartan officials—declared war on the helots annually, a move that absolved the Spartans in advance of any religious pollution they would incur should they wind up killing a helot or two over the course of the year. Spartan youths who showed especial promise, meanwhile, were periodically dispatched with daggers to stalk and kill helots—an institution called the *krypteia* (“time in hiding”), which served both as a means of policing the helot population and as a training exercise for the Spartans.[3]

The Spartans lived off the backs of their helots, but they paid a high price for the privilege. Because the helots far outnumbered Sparta’s citizen population, the Spartans lived in constant fear of helot revolt and needed to be always on their guard against the possibility. To that end, the Spartans adopted a lifestyle that most moderns would find unendurable. They devoted themselves to the practice of warfare to the exclusion of other pursuits. (Full Spartan citizens were in fact forbidden by law from engaging in other types of work.) At the age of seven Spartan boys were enrolled in the *agoge*, a brutal, compulsory educational system that emphasized discipline and endurance. They lived in communal barracks, were deliberately underfed to accustom them to hunger, and in general were toughened up so as to become uncomplaining, resilient cogs in the Spartan war machine. At the age of thirty successful graduates of the *agoge* became full Spartan citizens—called *homoioi* (“similar ones”) or Spartiates—but they continued to live austere lives, devoted to the common weal. So it was that the labors of their subject population freed the Spartans—but at the same time obliged them—to become a military state, Greece’s only professional standing army.[4]

Literally standing: the Spartans did have ships—they contributed sixteen to the allied fleet that fought at Salamis, for example—but they were at their best when waging war on foot, as hoplites. These were heavily armed soldiers who fought with spears and swords in rectangular formations called phalanxes. The citizens of other Greek city-states likewise fought in hoplite formation—the gear and technique were not specific to Sparta—but the Spartans trained for war more than anyone else in Greece, and they imbibed the Spartan warrior ethos with their mother's milk: never to yield in battle, but to conquer or die. They were in consequence the most formidable infantry Greece had to offer.[5]

Athens

Sparta had been a dominant military power in Greece for some time, but in the early fifth century Athens was just coming into its own. With the help of the Spartans, the Athenians had ousted their tyrant Hippias in 510. Political reforms introduced shortly afterwards left the polis a nascent democracy. In 499 the Athenians sent a fleet of twenty ships to help out when the Greek city-states in Asia Minor revolted against Persia. (These poleis, colonies of Athens and other city-states on the mainland, had been subsumed into the Persian Empire in the mid-sixth century.) The Athenians' involvement in the revolt was brief—just long enough for them to take part in burning the Persian capital of Sardis and to be badly defeated by the Persians in turn—but it was long enough to make an impression on Darius, Xerxes' father and predecessor on the throne. Nine years later a Persian armada crossed the Aegean with a view to punishing the Athenians. The Persians landed at Marathon, a plain in the northeast corner of Attica (the territory controlled by Athens), and against all odds were soundly defeated by the Athenians, whom they outnumbered by probably at least two to one. The Spartans, who had not managed to get to Marathon in time to help the Athenians, were impressed.[6]

Xerxes succeeded his father in 486 and, as we've seen, led an expedition by land and sea against all of Greece, not just Athens, in 480. Had he invaded just a few years earlier, things might have gone very differently. But as it happened, Athens—due to a stroke of good fortune and one man's keen foresight—had recently turned itself into a naval power. In 483 state-owned silver mines in southern Attica yielded a substantial surplus revenue. The Athenians were on the verge of voting to distribute the windfall equally among the citizenry, but a man named Themistocles, who may have been serving as one of Athens' generals that year, persuaded them to use the money instead to enlarge their fleet. He argued that the ships would come in handy against Aegina—an island in the Saronic Gulf that was a longtime commercial rival and enemy of Athens—but it's hard to believe that he wasn't also thinking of the looming threat from Persia. It was due to Themistocles' good counsel, at any rate, that the Athenians had a fleet of two hundred ships, the largest in Greece, by the time Xerxes invaded in 480.[7]

The Delian League

The Greek win at Salamis, then, was due largely to the Athenians. The Greeks would almost certainly have lost the battle without them, since Athens had contributed nearly half of the ships in the allied fleet. Victories on land—at Plataea, in central Greece, and at Mycale in Asia Minor—followed in 479. The Peloponnesians in the fleet sailed back home soon after the Battle of Mycale, but the Athenians decided to remain at sea a while longer and lay siege to Sestus, a city on the European side of the Hellespont that was still in Persian hands. The Athenians and the allies who were with them took Sestus after a few months, and that, for Herodotus, marked the end of the Second Persian War. He closes his *History* with an arresting image: the Athenians executed the Persian governor of Sestus by fastening him to a plank and hanging him up to die, this at the very spot, Herodotus says, where Xerxes had built one of his bridges and crossed the Hellespont into Europe.[8]

But even Sestus wasn't the end of it. The allies had driven Xerxes out of Greece and put a dent in his war machine, but Persia's king ruled over more than 10 percent of the planet: he would land on his feet. It was reasonable to assume that Xerxes would eventually attempt to conquer Greece again. In 478, therefore, the allied Greek fleet was back at it, this time taking the fight to the Persians, and their ships were once again under the leadership of a Spartan admiral: despite Athens' sizeable contribution to the fleet, the Greeks in the Hellenic League had decided early on to give Sparta the leadership of the allied forces, both by land and sea. Under the command of the Spartan Pausanias, the Greeks campaigned successfully against Cyprus and Byzantium, which the Persians still occupied. But the allies soon began to chafe under Pausanias's administration. This graduate of the Spartan *agoge* and hero of the battle at Plataea reportedly started going native—wearing Persian clothes and living grandly—and he was arrogant and even cruel to the allies. His behavior prompted the Spartans to recall him and made him so unpopular with the non-Peloponnesian Greeks that, in his absence, they wound up asking the Athenians to become their leaders instead. By the time the Spartans sent out a replacement for Pausanias it was a done deal: the Spartans were no longer needed. They appear to have accepted the allies' rejection gracefully: Athens was competent to carry on hostilities against the Persians, after all, and the Spartans were just as happy to be rid of the business. Pausanias' successor sailed back home.[9]

The allies' arrangement with Athens was soon formalized. They swore oaths upon joining the new league, and the Athenians assessed member contributions: allied states would either provide ships for continued operations against Persia or pay an annual tribute in cash. League operations would be conducted under Athenian commanders. The league treasury was to be kept on the small island of Delos in the Aegean, where the allies would also hold their meetings. Because of the island's role in league affairs, modern historians call the alliance the Delian League, though the ancients would have referred to it simply as "the Athenians and their allies." These allies included states from the islands and the coasts of the Aegean: unlike the Hellenic League, there were no Peloponnesians in this group.[10]

Under Athens' leadership the allies really did bring hostilities with Persia to an end. Over the next three decades the league confronted the king's forces throughout the eastern Mediterranean, but after Athens' victory in Cyprus in 451 or 450, we hear of no further fighting between Greeks and Persians. There may have been a formal treaty ending the hostilities and defining the belligerents' respective spheres of influence—the king in essence ceding the Aegean to Athenian control—or merely an informal understanding to the same effect, but whether de jure or de facto, the war against Persia was over. The Delian League, however, was still very much in existence.

The Athenian alliance had been created to continue hostilities against the Persians after Xerxes was driven out of Greece. Once that fight was seen to be over, whether it was concluded formally or informally, we might reasonably expect the league to have been disbanded or at least allowed to fall into quiescence. That it was not, that the allies were still expected to pay their annual tribute to Athens, was an important step in the alliance's metamorphosis: by the time hostilities with Persia had ceased, the league was well on its way to changing from a coalition of "autonomous allies who made decisions in joint congresses" into an Athenian empire. Twenty years later, in a speech before Athens' assembly, the Athenian statesman and general Pericles could reasonably liken the Delian League to a tyranny, with Athens its tyrant. By that point, the transformation of the alliance was complete.[11]

The Second Peloponnesian War

The Athenians spent the mid-fifth century pushing the Persians out of the Aegean and tightening their control over their allies in the Delian League. They also wound up fighting an on-again, off-again war with Sparta and her allies, a series of conflicts sometimes called the First Peloponnesian War (c. 460–445). This war ended in the winter of 446/5 with the ratification of the Thirty Years' Peace, an agreement that amounted to an acknowledgment of Athens' maritime empire. The Greek world was now patently divided into Spartan and Athenian blocs. Sparta remained the dominant power on land. Athens, having rid the Aegean of Persian warships, was the unrivaled master of the sea.

As its name suggests, the peace that ended the First Peloponnesian War was meant to remain in effect for thirty years. It lasted about half that. The Athenians and their allies and the Spartans and their allies were soon embroiled in a second war, which would consume the Greek world for twenty-seven years and permanently alter the area's geopolitical landscape. The Second Peloponnesian War (431–404) unfolded in three stages. The first ten years of the war were characterized by repeated Spartan invasions of Attica and Athenian raids on the Peloponnesian coast. This period was followed by an uneasy peace during which the Athenians undertook an ultimately disastrous expedition to Sicily. During the final phase of the war, the Spartans, now financed by Persia, attempted to undermine Athens' empire by supporting revolts among her allies in the Aegean and on the coast of Asia Minor. (The central part of Asia Minor was called Ionia, which is why historians sometimes refer to this period of hostilities as the Ionian War.) We'll discuss each of these phases more fully below.

The Ten Years' War

In the late summer of 432 the Spartans and their allies decided that Athens was guilty of violating the terms of the Thirty Years' Peace: the Athenians had fought a naval battle against the Corinthians, powerful allies of Sparta, off of Corcyra in western Greece, and they were besieging Potidaea, a Corinthian colony in the north Aegean. The allies voted for war, and in the following spring Sparta's king Archidamus led an allied army northeast out of the Peloponnese. When the Spartans got to Attica they set to wreaking havoc on the Athenian landscape—burning fields and chopping down vines and olive trees. The hope was that their devastation of property would provoke the Athenians into a confrontation on land in which the Spartans, with their dominant infantry, would have the upper hand. The plan didn't work. During this and subsequent incursions the Athenians evacuated their countryside and massed together, uncomfortable and disgruntled, inside their city's walls. It was not easy for Athens' temporarily dispossessed farmers to sit back and watch—sometimes quite literally—as the Spartans ravaged their fields, but they reined in their tempers and refused to be drawn into a battle they would almost certainly lose. Instead of meeting Sparta's infantry in Attica, the Athenians dispatched a fleet to sail around the Peloponnese and inflict damage where it could—the hoplites on board disembarking to take a town here or ravage a plain there.[12]

The Athenians' strategy of withdrawing behind their walls and refusing battle was the policy urged by Pericles, Athens' leading statesman at the time. Athens, because of its fortifications and its naval power, was in the singular position of being virtually impregnable to assault by land. Athens itself and its principal harbor area, the Piraeus, had been fortified with walls shortly after the Second Persian War (refortified, in the case of the city walls, which the Persians had destroyed). In the mid-fifth century, these walls were augmented by further fortifications, the so-called Long Walls, which stretched from Athens to the Piraeus wall in the north and to the port of Phalerum in the south, forming a wedge that encompassed all Athens' harbors. A third, middle wall was added later, south of and parallel to the north wall, creating a narrow corridor that linked Athens to the Piraeus. With these walls in place, the Athenians could gain access to the sea however many Spartan hoplites might be lying in wait outside them. Athens, that is, was a virtual island. As long as the Athenians retained control of the sea, and thus could import sufficient grain to feed their population, they could withstand a siege indefinitely. The Spartan invasions of Attica, then, while unpleasant for the Athenians to endure, could not be decisive on their own.[13]

There was, however, an unforeseen consequence of Pericles' island strategy. The overcrowding in Athens during these periods of withdrawal was not only unpleasant but, more importantly, it was unsanitary. The area encompassed by Athens' fortifications was not large enough to accommodate another hundred thousand or more people comfortably. The evacuees made do in makeshift shacks or camped out in temples, and they created a mountain of excess garbage and sewage. The result was an "enormous and squalid refugee camp," as Victor Hanson writes, which proved fertile ground when the plague struck in 430. This disease, which has never been conclusively identified, was brought in by boat—not surprising, given that Athens had commercial contacts throughout the Mediterranean. It first appeared in the Piraeus and made its way up the walls to the city proper. The illness was often fatal—those who contracted it usually died after seven or eight days—and it was horrible in its effects. Thucydides describes the plague in his *History of the Peloponnesian War* and lists a gruesome litany of its symptoms: ineffectual retching, pustules and ulcers, coughing, insomnia, unquenchable thirst and fetid breath, severe diarrhea. Those who survived sometimes suffered the loss of their fingers and toes, their vision, their memory. The plague killed an estimated one-third of Athens' population—including Pericles—significantly reducing the city's military ranks. That the Athenians managed to continue fighting a war despite suffering such losses is remarkable.[14]

The Spartans invaded Attica five times between 431 and 425. In 429, the third year of the war, they opted to invade the territory of Boeotia instead, probably because they were unwilling to get too close to Athens, where plumes of smoke were constantly rising from the funeral pyres of plague victims. In 426 they were about to invade and had advanced as far as the Isthmus of Corinth when an earthquake made them turn around: natural disasters could provide the helots with an opportunity to revolt from their Spartan masters.[15]

The Spartans might have persevered indefinitely with their (more or less) annual invasions of Attica had something not happened—midinvasion, in fact—to put an end to them. In the spring of 425, the enterprising Athenian general Demosthenes, when Athens' fleet was driven ashore by a storm, wound up fortifying and holding a place called Pylos, a promontory on the west coast of the Peloponnese. This permanent occupation of a position in enemy territory was a departure from Athens' usual hit-and-run tactics. Pylos could now serve as a base for continual attacks on the Peloponnese and, more frightening yet for the Spartans, as a refuge for rebellious helots. The Spartan army that was in Attica at the time quit its ravaging and hurried home to deal with the crisis. An unsuccessful assault on Demosthenes' position followed, then an Athenian blockade of the Spartans' position on Sphacteria, an island opposite Pylos. Seventy-two days into the blockade, the Athenians defeated the Spartans in battle, killing 128 of them. The rest wound up surrendering—a result that shocked the Greek world. (The general feeling was that the Spartans—those quintessential warriors whose ancestors had perished to a man trying to hold the pass at Thermopylae—would never surrender their arms but would "die with them in their hands.") The Athenians took 292 men hostage, about 120 of whom were full Spartan citizens. Athens' custody of these high-value hostages put an end to the Spartans' annual incursions: the Athenians had threatened to execute the prisoners if Attica was invaded again.[16]

The occupation of Pylos was a high point in the war for Athens. The Spartans sued for peace repeatedly afterwards, but the Athenians rejected their overtures, demanding more concessions from their weakened enemy than the Spartans were prepared to give. Other successes followed, but by 421 the Athenians were smarting from heavy losses sustained in a battle at Delium in Boeotia and from the loss of Amphipolis, a strategically important city in the north Aegean: Amphipolis supplied Athens with timber necessary for shipbuilding, and it commanded the bridge over the Strymon River. The Spartans' possession of the place would allow them access to Athens' allies to the east and might also eventually imperil Athens' grain supply. Even during times of peace, Athens depended on supplementing her locally grown wheat and barley with grain imported from the Black Sea area. The Athenians' control of the grain route through the Hellespont and Bosporus was thus vitally important.[17]

In 421, with both sides eager to get something back from the enemy, the Spartans and Athenians swore to a defensive alliance and to the Peace of Nicias—named after the Athenian general who, together with Sparta's king Pleistonax, was largely responsible for negotiating its terms. Broadly speaking, the peace stipulated that the Athenians and Spartans were to release any prisoners of war in their custody and to restore the territories they had acquired through conquest (with a couple of exceptions) during the previous ten years. This means that the Athenians finally freed the Spartans they had captured on Sphacteria in 425. The Spartans, for their part, promised to return Amphipolis to Athens. Their failure to do so was one reason why the peace ultimately failed.[18]

Thucydides called the first ten years of the Second Peloponnesian War the Ten Years' War, but since at least the fourth century B.C. it has often been referred to as the Archidamian War, after Sparta's king Archidamus, who led the first three Spartan invasions into Attica. The nomenclature is ironic both because Archidamus died in 427, only a few years into the conflict, and because he had opposed the war from the get-go. At a meeting of the Spartan assembly in 432 he urged his countrymen to pursue a diplomatic solution with Athens before leaping into armed conflict. As Thucydides tells the story, even before the first spear was raised, Archidamus had recognized a fundamental truth that would bear on the conduct of the war, one that we have emphasized here more than once: Sparta was a land power, and Athens a naval power that could import what it needed by sea. The Spartans could not win the war against

Athens unless they put a stop to the Athenian fleet, either by developing a naval arm capable of defeating it or by depriving the Athenians of the revenue that supported it.[19]

The Sicilian Expedition

The Peace of Nicias was doomed from the start. A number of Sparta's allies refused to agree to it, Sparta could not or would not return Amphipolis to Athens, and the Athenians in turn refused to return Pylos to Sparta. Thus the terms of the agreement were violated almost immediately. The peace remained in effect nonetheless for almost seven years, but it was an uneasy peace at best. The Athenians continued to raid the coast of the Peloponnese during this time. They installed former helots in Pylos so that they could ravage the western Peloponnese. And, most dramatically, the Athenians and Spartans fought on opposite sides in a major pitched battle at Mantinea in the Peloponnese in 418. Given how unsatisfactory a peace this peace was, a renewal of open hostilities was surely inevitable.[20]

During this period of instability in Greece, the Athenians decided to send an expedition west to Sicily when their allies the Egestaeans came asking for help in their war against a neighboring state, Selinus, and its ally, Syracuse. The Athenians, whose recent losses from the plague and the war with Sparta should have made them more cautious about risking their men and ships, were nonetheless fired up for the campaign, which promised adventure, riches, and, perhaps, access to Sicily's grain supply. The Athenians expected the campaign to be safe because the force they were dispatching was so large: 134 triremes (warships)—100 of them Athenian—were launched in the summer of 415. These would have been manned by more than twenty-five thousand men—allies, mercenaries, and the Athenians themselves. As many boats again accompanied the fleet, carrying supplies and nonmilitary personnel. This magnificent armada was the most expensive and most splendid force a single Greek city had ever assembled. Even so, the Athenians later supplemented it with more than 80 additional ships and some eighteen thousand more men.[21]

The Athenians might have foreseen that undertaking such a large expedition so far from home while their relations with the Spartans were precarious was unwise. It was in fact Sparta that proved the Athenians' undoing in Sicily. In the summer of 414, the Spartans sent a small fleet west to try to prevent the Athenians from capturing Syracuse. They also sent out a general, Gylippus, to take command of the Peloponnesian and Syracusan forces in Sicily.

The Syracusans, who had been on the verge of coming to terms with the Athenians, rallied when they heard the Spartans were en route. Under Gylippus's leadership they soon won their first major victory against the Athenians, on land. Before long they would be confident enough to challenge their enemy also at sea.[22]

In the following spring, back in Greece, the Spartans took another bold step against Athens. They marched into Attica and fortified a place called Decelea, which lay about fourteen miles northeast of Athens. The Spartans now had a fort in Athenian territory, comparable to the Athenians' fort at Pylos, from which they could launch raids year-round, disrupting life in the Attic countryside, exhausting the Athenians with the need to be constantly on alert, and providing a haven for runaway slaves.[23] The Peace of Nicias, which of course forbad this sort of thing, was now well and truly broken. Nicias himself, who had brokered the peace back in 421 and who was now serving as one of Athens' generals in Sicily, would soon be just as defunct.

The Sicilian Expedition ended in the winter of 413 with the total defeat of Athens' forces. In the end, every trireme the Athenians had dispatched to Sicily was either destroyed or captured, and the men themselves were nearly all killed or enslaved. During the Athenians' final retreat overland—a vain, last-ditch effort to save themselves after their fleet had been defeated in Syracuse's harbor—Nicias finally surrendered to the Spartan general Gylippus. He told the Spartans they could do what they liked with him as long as they stopped the slaughter of his men. The Spartans started taking prisoners, and a bit later the Syracusans, over Gylippus's objections, slit Nicias's throat.[24]

The Ionian War (to the Battle of Notium)

The expedition to Sicily was a disaster for the Athenians, a wholly avoidable debacle that left them much weakened in manpower, ships, and prestige: they and their allies had lost 216 ships and some forty thousand men in Sicily in a little more than two years. On top of that, the war with Sparta was back on, the Spartans were camped out year-round in Attica, the Athenians' treasury was severely depleted, their slaves were deserting to Decelea willy-nilly, and Athens' "allies," seeing the Athenians weakened by their losses, were ripe for revolt.[25]

A number of states around the Aegean began intriguing with the Spartans soon after the Athenians' defeat, looking for Peloponnesian support before they broke away from Athens. The Spartans responded by sending a small fleet out to the Aegean the following spring. Its arrival sparked a rash of revolts among cities on the coast of Asia Minor and on the nearby islands, chief among them Chios, which joined the Spartans in instigating other rebellions. The revolt of Chios was a particularly devastating blow for Athens because the Chians brought a substantial fleet of sixty ships to the Spartan cause.[26]

Before dispatching their fleet, the Spartans had mapped out a two-part plan of attack. First they would attempt to disrupt Athens' naval empire by stirring up revolts among her allies in the Aegean. Then they would focus on the Hellespont, control of which, as we've mentioned, was vitally important to the Athenians because of their dependence on imported grain. Given how bleak things looked for Athens after the failure in Sicily, the Spartans can be forgiven for thinking that Athenian power would soon collapse. But they, and Athens' allies who rose in revolt, seriously underestimated the Athenians' ability to hold out. Even after their losses in Sicily, the Athenians could still put about a hundred ships in the water, a force roughly equal to what the Spartans had at their disposal once they'd joined forces with Chios. The Athenians spent 412 and 411 responding to the revolts of their allies, but no great actions took place that upset the status quo. The Aegean phase of the Spartans' plan resulted in stalemate.[27]

The Spartans were not the only ones looking to undermine the Athenian empire during this period. Back in the winter of 413/12, when Athens' allies went to Sparta looking for help with their revolts, the Spartans were also approached by emissaries from two important Persians. One of these was Tissaphernes, who seems to have held a military command over western Asia Minor. He wanted the Spartans to send a fleet against Athens' allies in the eastern Aegean. Ultimately he wanted the Greek cities in Asia to be returned to Persian control, as they had been prior to the Second Persian War. In return Tissaphernes offered to maintain Sparta's forces. The second Persian who sent ambassadors to the Spartans was Pharnabazus, the Persian governor of Dascylium, just south of the Sea of Marmara. He offered to fund Spartan military action against Athenian allies in the Hellespont area, likewise in order to recover those cities for the Persian king.[28] The Spartans had opted to work with Tissaphernes first, sending a fleet out to Asia Minor and Chios in the spring of 412. Tissaphernes, however, was not as forthcoming with his cash as the Spartans would have liked. The pay he provided was irregular and insufficient. Tissaphernes also kept claiming that a Phoenician fleet would arrive and help the Spartans at sea—an increase in their forces that would probably have been decisive in ending the war—but the fleet never materialized. In the spring of 411, the

Spartans had begun sending land and naval forces to the Hellespont, where they set about raising rebellions among Athens' allies. Now, with Tissaphernes shirking his financial obligations and the promised Phoenician fleet a no-show, and with Pharnabazus, the Spartans' second Persian suitor, ready to furnish pay, the Spartans leapt more fully into the second phase of their plan. In September or October of 411 they moved most of the ships they still had in the eastern Aegean up to Abydus on the Hellespont, making a grand total there of eighty-six triremes.[29]

The Spartans' presence in the Hellespont forced the Athenians to move north as well. They sailed to the strait with seventy-six ships and promptly won two battles against the Spartans, at Cynossema and Abydus. These were followed in the spring of 410 by a third Athenian victory, at Cyzicus. This last battle was a game changer—at least potentially. The Athenians not only recovered Cyzicus from the Spartans, they crushed the Peloponnesian fleet in one blow, destroying or capturing all of the ships the Spartans had in the Hellespont. This might have meant the end of Sparta's efforts to undermine Athens' Aegean empire, but the Spartans had an ace in the hole: their Persian friend Pharnabazus was more than happy to finance the reconstruction of a Spartan fleet. Pharnabazus ordered that ships be built at once to replace those the Spartans had lost.[30]

Although the Athenians had scored a major victory against the Spartans at Cyzicus, they didn't have the money or the manpower needed to fully exploit their win. A stronger Athens could have set to work with vigor on the tasks that needed doing: regaining the territory they'd lost in the Hellespont and the Aegean and rebuilding their fleet. It took them years, however, just to recover most of the cities they had lost in the Hellespont. It wasn't until 407 that the area was finally secure enough for them to send most of their fleet home to Athens.[31]

With the Hellespont for the most part under their control, the Athenians soon turned to the next task on their list: driving the Spartans out of the Aegean. In October of 407 they sent a fleet of one hundred ships out to Ionia. Twenty triremes appear to have been left at Andros en route, so the Athenians had eighty ships when they established themselves at Samos, their base of operations in the Aegean. The Spartans, who had likewise been recovering their strength over the previous three years, had ninety ships stationed at Ephesus, just north of Samos on the coast of Asia Minor. The Athenians, in other words, no longer enjoyed an overwhelming advantage over the Spartans at sea, and, unlike the Spartans, they weren't being bankrolled by a benign superpower. A single defeat could be enough to ruin them: the stakes in the Aegean were as high as they'd ever been.[32]

Two important personnel changes occurred in 407 that bolstered the Spartans' position. Early in the year the Spartans dispatched a new navarch (naval commander) to take charge of their fleet. Lysander would turn out to be a particularly competent and ambitious admiral who, unusually for a Spartan, also excelled at diplomacy. Certainly he was able to successfully woo Cyrus, the fifteen- or sixteen-year-old son of the Persian king, who had been sent to the Aegean to serve as the commander of Persia's forces in western Asia Minor. The two met in Sardis and hit it off. Cyrus was eager to help the Spartans win the war, and he had deeper pockets than Pharnabazus. He agreed to increase the pay of Lysander's sailors by a third—from three obols a day, which is what the Athenians were paying their oarsmen, to four. It was Lysander's hope that the higher wages he could offer would induce the mercenaries serving in Athens' fleet to desert and seek employment instead on his ships.[33]

Lysander had the enthusiastic backing of the king's son, and he was offering wages that would likely induce Athens' mercenaries to start defecting en masse. Delay, under these circumstances, could only make matters worse for the Athenians. With a view to luring Lysander into a battle sooner rather than later, they sailed up to the harbor at Ephesus, but Lysander didn't take the bait. The Athenians withdrew and anchored nearby at the port of Notium, where they waited for the Spartans to take to the water and offer battle. After a time, however—it's not clear how long the Athenians delayed at Notium—a contingent of Athenian ships sailed away under the command of the Athenian general Alcibiades. While Alcibiades was away, and against his express orders, a small number of the Athenian ships left behind at Notium challenged the enemy—precisely what happened and why is a little murky—and Lysander grabbed his opportunity. In the battle that followed the Athenians lost fifteen or twenty-two ships, depending on which ancient source you believe, and Alcibiades, who was held responsible for the defeat, lost his job.[34]

The Siege of Mytilene

In the spring of 406 the Athenians held their annual elections and voted in a new board of ten generals. Some of the men who were serving in the Aegean in 407 were reelected to the generalship, but Alcibiades was not among them. He sailed off to a property he owned on the Chersonese, where he would henceforth watch the war from afar. The historian Xenophon provides a complete list of the generals elected in 406: Conon, Leon, Archestratus, Erasinides, Diomedon, Aristocrates, Protomachus, Thrasyllus, Aristogenes, and Pericles (the son of the statesman and general Pericles, who had died earlier in the war from the plague). The careers of most of these men would soon be ending in ignominy.[35]

There were changes in the Spartan leadership as well. Lysander's stint as navarch ended in the spring of 406. Callicratidas, his replacement, took over the fleet, fitted out another fifty triremes, and was soon headed for Lesbos with 140 ships. The Athenians were now seriously outnumbered. They had more than a hundred ships at Samos, but they may not have had enough oarsmen to man them all. When they heard that Callicratidas was attacking the city of Methymna on Lesbos, they sailed north with only seventy triremes. These were commanded by four of Athens' generals—Conon, Leon, Archestratus, and Erasinides. Unfortunately, Conon and his colleagues were too late: by the time they got there, Methymna had already been taken.[36]

Having failed to save Methymna, the Athenians put in at Arginusae, a cluster of islands off the coast of Asia Minor opposite Lesbos. It was there, probably, that Conon received a message from Callicratidas: the Spartan navarch threatened that he would "stop Conon committing *moicheia* with the sea." *Moicheia* is often translated as "adultery," but that isn't quite accurate: a *moichos* was a male who had sex with a woman who was under another man's protection—his wife or daughter or even his mother. What Callicratidas was saying, then, was that the Athenians' relationship with the sea was illicit, and that the Aegean properly belonged to the Spartan state. Probably he was hoping his insult would provoke Conon into doing something stupid, like forming up for battle against a fleet that was twice the size of his. But Conon wasn't about to be lured into an unfair contest if he could help it.[37]

In the morning the Athenians put to sea, probably intending to head back to Samos, but Callicratidas sailed out and cut them off. The Athenians fled instead toward Mytilene on Lesbos. Our sources disagree on what happened during the chase that followed, but whatever the particulars, the Athenians' flight ended in a battle in the mouth of Mytilene's harbor. The result was terrible: only forty of Athens' seventy ships made it to safety. The rest were captured by the Spartans, who now blockaded Mytilene by land and sea. The Athenian general Archestratus seems to have been among those killed in the battle.[38]

The danger Athens now faced can hardly be overstated. The Athenians had only 40 ships in Lesbos against their enemy's 170 (30 captured ships having now been added to the original Spartan fleet).[39] They were under siege, trapped in a city that might be betrayed to the Spartans at virtually any moment. If Mytilene was captured, the Athenians would lose their fleet, and the Spartans would be masters of the sea, with all that implied: Athens would lose her allies in the Aegean and the Hellespont, and the Spartans would control the grain route from the Black Sea, enabling them to starve the Athenians into submission whenever it suited them. The Athenians back home, meanwhile, had no idea what had happened at Lesbos, so they wouldn't be sending help. Alerting them was perhaps the fleet's only hope: if more ships could be sent to Lesbos before Mytilene fell, Athens might yet survive this crisis.

In order to get a message to Athens the generals needed to slip a ship past the Spartans' blockade. They settled on a clever stratagem. They selected two of their fastest triremes, manned them with the best oarsmen, and hid marines in the ships' hulls. The vessels went out into the harbor every day for four days, and they returned to shore every evening. The idea, apparently, was to make it appear that the ships were on guard duty rather than looking for a chance to escape: the Spartans would become accustomed to seeing them on the water and might eventually become careless. At midday on the fifth day, when the Spartans' guard was down, the two ships, now also carrying a supply of food, suddenly made a run for it. One of the ships, which Leon seems to have been commanding, rowed out of the harbor toward the open sea. The other, with Erasinides on board, fled north toward the Hellespont. The Spartans were caught with their pants down—some of them probably literally. They had been eating lunch on shore and now rushed to man their ships and give chase. Many hours of strenuous rowing later, when the sun was slipping below the horizon, they finally caught up to Leon's trireme: they captured the ship and its crew and brought them back to their camp. But for some reason the Spartans had not pursued the Athenian ship that fled north. That trireme made it safely to Athens to deliver its message: the Athenians' help was urgently needed in Lesbos.[40]

-II-

Naval Warfare: Ramming, Dying, and Breaking Wind at Sea

It is hard to imagine any activity in the ancient world, and perhaps in the modern, which has required the simultaneous exercise of such a high level of skill from so large a group of people.

Boris Rankov, "Rowing Olympias: A Matter of Skill"

AFTER A QUARTER CENTURY of brutal warfare it came to this: thirty-eight Athenian ships—about half the vessels Athens had in the Aegean—were trapped in Mytilene. Their enemies were laying siege to the city, cutting the Athenians off from help or escape overland, and a Spartan fleet that outnumbered the Athenians' by more than four to one was guarding the harbor. Still, a pair of triremes had slipped through the Spartan blockade, and one of them had managed to elude capture and ply its way across the sea to Athens.

Before we get to Athens, however, and the hubbub of activity that the trireme's arrival inspired, I'd like to pause and consider what precisely it meant to "ply one's way" across the sea in a trireme in 406 B.C. Back in 480, the Athenians had established themselves as a dominant power in Greece by defeating the Persians at sea off the coast of Salamis. They had since won their empire, and would soon lose it, on the sea. The engine of Athens' domination was the trireme. To better understand Athenian history, and in particular the battle that will be the subject of our next chapter, it's worth taking a closer look at this vessel, how it operated, how it fought, and what conditions were like for those on board.

The Trireme

Triremes were the state-of-the-art warships of the classical period. These wooden ships could travel under sail, but much of the time—and always during battle—they were powered by rowers. The trireme's flanks bristled with oars, 170 of them in all, each about fifteen feet long. Eighty-five oars projected from either side of the vessel in three levels—31 in the top row, and 27 in each of the two lower rows. The ship's 170 oarsmen—each oar was pulled by a single rower—were likewise seated in three tiers. The prefix *tri* in *trireme* (*trieres* in ancient Greek) may refer to these three levels of rowers, whom we'll be hearing more about shortly.

In addition to the ship's oarsmen, there were some thirty other personnel on board. Typically, a trireme carried ten hoplites, who stayed on deck and served as marines (*epibatai*), and four archers (*toxotai*). There was also a ship's captain (trierarch), a helmsman (*kybernetes*), a rowing master (*keleustes*), a purser (*pentekontarchos*), a ship's carpenter (*naupegos*), a piper (*auletes*), and a bow officer (*prorates*). The remaining ten crew members may have served as general-purpose workers—managing the sails or bailing the ship or filling in as spare

Figure 1. The trireme *Olympias* under oar in 1987 off of the Peloponnese.
© The Trireme Trust

rowers as needed. Triremes could be used as troop carriers to ferry armies from one place to another. In that case each vessel could carry another thirty men in addition to its regular complement. But under normal circumstances a trireme would have had about two hundred men on board.[1]

Triremes were built for speed and maneuverability. They were long and thin, about 120 feet by 18 feet. (That's roughly the length of a tennis court with its surrounding clear space, but only a third of the width: three triremes parked abreast could just fit on the grass at Wimbledon's Centre Court.) With oars extended, of course, the trireme's footprint more than doubled in width. For short bursts a trireme could reach a top speed of 9 or 10 nautical miles per hour (or knots), which is the equivalent of 10.4 to 11.5 land miles per hour. (One nautical mile is roughly equal to 1.15 land miles.) For longer periods it was possible to maintain a speed of 7 to 8 knots.[2]

Triremes were equipped with a bronze-clad wooden ram, which extended about six and a half feet from the prow of the vessel at waterline and ended in three horizontal cutting blades. These were reinforced by a central vertical support, so head on the tip of the ram looked like an I-beam bisected by a third horizontal bar. In profile the ram looked like the business end of a giant shrimp fork (see fig. 2). Although triremes could be used for other purposes—as dispatch boats or troop carriers or, when converted, horse transports—their principal function was to disable enemy ships during battle by ramming them. In

Figure 2. The trireme *Olympias* in drydock, with a good view of the cutting blades on the ship's bronze ram. © User:Templar52 /Wikimedia Commons/ http://commons.wikimedia.org/wiki /File:Olympias.1.JPG

order to perform this task well they needed to be able to accelerate and back water quickly and to make fast, tight turns.

The quality of a trireme's crew—their physical condition and their experience working together as a team—was a major factor in the ship's performance. But even a top-notch crew could only do so much if their vessel was inherently slow. Regular maintenance was required for triremes to remain in peak condition. Perhaps every two or three months a ship had to be hauled out of the water and allowed to dry thoroughly (which might take days or weeks), as its wooden hull would become waterlogged and rough with marine growths, both of which would slow the ship down. Once dry, the ship could be scraped and recaulked and recoated with pitch. The speed and maneuverability of a trireme also depended on how much weight it was carrying. A ship would necessarily be slower and less agile if it was ferrying around extra men or supplies.[3]

There was very little storage room on a trireme, space being at a minimum on a ship that was built to be as light as possible. In particular, although each rower probably had a water-skin stowed somewhere near his seat, triremes could not carry more than a few days' worth of food, if that. On long trips a trireme's crew would need to either rendezvous with an accompanying supply ship or go ashore and buy food from a market in a friendly city. Meanwhile, even if there was food on board, conditions were so cramped that preparing and eating it on the ship would have been an unpleasant prospect. Instead, sailors regularly went ashore to eat, leaving their ships at anchor while they did so.

Thucydides mentions a notable exception to this practice in his account of the revolt of Mytilene on Lesbos. After the Athenians had suppressed the revolt in 427, the assembly, back in Athens, voted to execute all the men in the city and to sell the women and children into slavery. They dispatched a trireme to bring orders to that effect to Paches, their general in Mytilene (a trip of about 184 nautical miles). The next day, however, the Athenians changed their minds: they decided to spare the innocent and execute only those Mytileneans whom they believed to be guilty of fomenting the rebellion. They immediately sent out another ship to catch up with the first, which by now had a roughly twenty-four-hour head start. The crew of the second ship made every effort to get to Lesbos in time: "Their haste was such that they ate while rowing, barley cakes mixed with wine and olive oil, and they slept and rowed by turns." In the end, they barely made it: Paches had read out the Athenians' decree, which the first ship had just delivered, and he was about to start executing people when the second ship arrived and prevented a massacre. The point of the story for our purposes is that, while eating on a trireme was possible, it was not standard procedure, and it would likely have been done only in special circumstances.[4] The trireme crews' need to eat and sleep on land had implications for how naval operations were conducted. Triremes typically sailed along the shore (or, in the Aegean, from island to island) rather than across open water. That way they could make landfall once or twice a day at spots where the crews could get fresh water, eat, and rest. Ideally the fleet would stop in friendly territory. When that wasn't possible, the crews would need to set guards and take precautions against an attack by land. But going ashore and letting the men run off to buy victuals at the nearest market left a fleet vulnerable even if the ships were anchored in territory they controlled. We hear more than once of fleets attacking an enemy's ships while their crews were off procuring or preparing a meal. Similarly, as we've seen, Conon's two triremes managed to slip out of Mytilene while the Spartans blockading the harbor were on shore having lunch.[5]

Another factor that influenced naval operations was the inability of triremes to operate well in rough weather. Strong winds and choppy seas made it difficult for a trireme's oarsmen to maintain their cohesion, and rowing into the wind would quickly exhaust a crew. The lowest level of rowers in the trireme had a particularly hard time in bad weather because of their position deep in the ship's hull: depending on the height of the waves and the cant of the ship, a large percentage of their oar shafts might be under water. Ships that were in close formation, meanwhile, could easily fall foul of one another in rough weather, the oars of one ship interfering with those of another. Simply trying to navigate from place to place under such conditions was difficult enough. Controlling a trireme with the precision required to execute complicated battle maneuvers verged on the impossible. If a storm arose, the wisest course for a fleet was to get to shelter as quickly as possible.[6]

The consequences of not seeking shelter in a storm could be dire. Our sources routinely mention fleets being delayed, rendered unmanageable, or destroyed outright by storms. A Persian fleet of three hundred ships was wrecked in a storm off Mount Athos in the north Aegean in 492, for example. Twenty-thousand men were lost, drowned or battered against the rocky coast or eaten by sharks. A pair of storms likewise destroyed many hundreds of ships in the Persian armada that came to conquer Greece a dozen years later. Less dramatically, the Athenian general Demosthenes wound up fortifying Pylos in 425 because a storm detained his fleet there: as we've seen, the Athenians' occupation of Pylos ultimately put an end to the Spartans' annual invasions of Attica. Because triremes were so affected by it, the weather could play a significant role in naval operations: indeed, a well-timed storm could change the course of history.[7]

Triremes were, in essence, man-powered, floating missiles—long and thin and tipped with a serrated beak, whose sole purpose was to punch a hole in the side of another ship. Doing this well was the art of ancient naval warfare—chasing down and ramming an enemy while avoiding being rammed oneself, 170 men pulling or backing water in unison with the din of battle full in their ears: the splashing of thousands of oar blades in a choppy surf, the creaking hull and pipers piping and orders shouted and now and then a crash as ram splintered wood, the screams of the dying. For most of the fifth century, the Athenians were unparalleled in their ability to destroy enemy ships in the midst of such pandemonium.

The *Olympias* Project

We said above that triremes were about 120 feet long, but we don't have any direct evidence for that statistic. No remains of a trireme have ever been found—in part because the ships were so buoyant that they didn't tend to sink to the bottom of the sea. (Instead, disabled ships filled with water and drifted around, half submerged. After a battle they were usually towed to shore for repair or salvage.) Nor has any ancient author left behind a detailed description of a trireme, let alone blueprints. Our understanding of the vessel rests, therefore, on indirect evidence: passing references to triremes in literary sources, representations of the ship on vase paintings and coins and in sculptural reliefs, inferences that can be made from the remains of other ships of the period that, unlike triremes, *did* sink.

Three other sources of indirect information about triremes are worth mentioning. First, the ram of an ancient warship was found in 1980 off the coast of Athlit in Israel. The Athlit ram is too heavy to have come from a trireme and must instead have fitted on some larger type of ship, and it probably dates to the third or fourth century B.C. rather than the fifth. But the ram nonetheless provides useful information relevant to the construction and mounting of fifth-century trireme rams. Second, a number of inscribed inventories dating to the fourth century B.C. were discovered in the Piraeus beginning in 1834, during the excavation of a late Roman or Byzantine-era portico. The inventories were published on stone annually and contain lists of the ships and equipment that were in the dockyards when the officials who supervised Athens' naval bases handed the job over to a new board. The lists provide information in particular about the number and length of the oars that a trireme of the period would have carried. In other words, these inscriptions are the reason we know that triremes were rowed by 170 men. Finally, to return to the point with which this section began, we know that triremes were about 120 feet long because of another archaeological find. Ship-sheds that were built to house Athens' triremes were excavated at Zea, one of the ports of the Piraeus, in the 1880s. Just as archaeologists of the future might deduce the size of early twenty-first-century automobiles from the remains of contemporary garages, the foundations of the Zea ship-sheds provide us with the maximum length and width of the vessels they were built to house: triremes could be no larger than, and were surely somewhat smaller than, 121 feet 5 inches by 19 feet 6 inches.[8]

After triremes fell out of use (the last battle in which they are known to have fought took place in A.D. 323), the knowledge of how they were constructed was lost. In particular, scholars puzzled for centuries over how the trireme's oar system had operated: the crew might have been sitting three men to an oar, for example, or three to a bench, with each man pulling his own oar. But by the mid-twentieth century it was generally agreed that the rowers were arranged in three tiers, each man pulling his own oar, which was the same length as those of the oarsmen above or below him. That was the theory, anyway. But could this theoretical system be made to work in real life?

In the early 1980s John Morrison, a historian and expert on ancient oared ships, together with naval architect John Coates and Frank Welsh, a banker and author, decided to embark on the project of building a full-scale reconstruction of a Greek trireme. Some years later Coates completed his design of the ship, which was then constructed in Greece and launched in 1987 by the Hellenic Navy as a commissioned warship. For the first time in more than fifteen hundred years a trireme, christened the *Olympias*, was plying the wine-dark waters of the Aegean. (In 1993, for the first time ever, a trireme would sail up the River Thames, when the *Olympias* was shipped to London to participate in a celebration of the 2500th anniversary of the birth of democracy.)[9]

Between 1987 and 1994 the *Olympias* underwent five seasons of trials at sea, during which the operation of the ship was tested—for example, her speed, acceleration, turning radius, and stability in winds. The highest speed the *Olympias* achieved under oar was 8.9 knots, an impressive performance, though it falls short of what ancient triremes are believed to have been capable of. The shortcoming is probably due partly to flaws in the ship's design and partly to the inexperience of the crews manning her. But certainly the performance of the *Olympias* has proved conclusively that the three-tiered system of oars adopted in her design is inherently viable.

In addition to testing the design and mechanics of the ship, the sea trials of the *Olympias* also served as a practical exploration of the experience of an ancient trireme's crew. The modern crew—volunteer oarsmen, both male and female, enlisted from around the world—faced many of the same problems that would have confronted their ancient counterparts: cramped quarters and sore buttocks, broken oars, the stench of the hold. Rowing the *Olympias* can't have been a perfect simulation of the real thing: the dimensions of the ship are probably not quite right, for one thing, and we moderns are at any rate larger on average than the ancient Greeks were;[10] the *Olympias*, moreover, didn't engage in battle. But short of time travel, the experience of those who rowed the *Olympias* is as good an approximation as we're likely to get of what it was like to serve on an ancient trireme. Our next section, on the experience of a trireme's oarsmen, will be informed by information gleaned from the *Olympias* trials.

Figures 1, 2, and 3 in this book show the *Olympias* under oar and in dry dock, while figure 4, which shows the ship's crew sitting at oar in three tiers, gives a good sense of the vessel's cramped interior. But if these pictures are worth a thousand words apiece, moving pictures are even more valuable. Videos of the sweatband-wreathed crew of the *Olympias* rowing off the coast of the Peloponnese bring alive the experience of the oarsmen in a way that still shots and literary references simply cannot. I highly recommend that interested readers give these videos a look:

— "Sea Trials of the Trireme Olympias" (14:17), posted by BRLSI
http://www.youtube.com/watch?v=ZcsrNrRkQis
— "Trireme Olympias" (2:39), posted by TriremeInNYC
http://www.youtube.com/watch?v=7da52cJLwW8
— "Trireme Olympias on Patrol" (7:50), posted by TriremeInNYC
http://www.youtube.com/watch?v=d4Dd5v_NHCs
— "The Trireme Dreadnought of the Ancient Mediterranean" (13:33), posted by HistoryCollaborative
http://www.youtube.com/watch?v=5e1cmprH6BY

The Oarsmen

As we said above, the 170 rowers who powered an ancient trireme were seated in three levels on either side of the ship, each man pulling his own oar. The sixty-two oarsmen in the topmost level—called thranites ("stool-sitters")[11]—

Figure 3. The top level of starboard oarsmen in the trireme *Olympias*, under oar in 1988. The oarholes of the zygians and thalamians are beneath them, the latter not far above the waterline. © The Trireme Trust

sat above the hull and under a removable wooden canopy, or deck, in an outrigger that extended beyond the side of the trireme. If you look at figure 3, which shows the starboard side of the *Olympias* under oar, the rowers that you see—the ones with the window seats—are the thranites. The other two levels of rowers sat below and inboard of them (see fig. 4). The fifty-four rowers on the middle level were the zygians, who sat on or near the beams (*zyga*) that crossed the ship. Those on the lowest level were the fifty-four thalamians, who sat in the ship's hold (*thalamos*).

Of the three groups of rowers, the thranites were by far the most comfortably situated. They had the best view among the oarsmen of what was going on inside the ship, and they were the only rowers able to look outside and see their oars hit the water, which made it easier for them to time their strokes. Add to that a cooling breeze off the Aegean and doubtless some magnificent views, and their position must have seemed downright idyllic to their colleagues on the lower benches. The zygians, inboard of and a bit lower than the thranites, were able to see along the inside of the ship, but they could not see their oar blades. In the middle level as they were, the zygians also had a middling experience: not as pleasant as what the thranites enjoyed, but far better than what the thalamians endured.

The thalamians, then, in the ship's hold, had the least enviable position of all. Their view within the ship was obstructed by the beams crossing the hull and by the bodies of the zygians, whose buttocks would have been roughly at eye level. Sweat from the upper levels of rowers dripped onto the thalamians and into the hold of the ship, where it became rank: the hull of the *Olympias,* John Morrison reports, had to be washed out with sea water every few days because of the stench of accumulated sweat.[12] There was little ventilation within the hold—none of those breezes the thranites were enjoying—so the thalamians sat dripping with their own and other men's sweat in the cramped, smelly, airless hold, unable to see very much, aware that if the vessel was rammed they were the most likely to be injured in the collision and to drown before being able to escape from the ship.

It must be added that the aforementioned zygian buttocks may have added untold horrors to the experience of the thalamians—or so the comic playwright Aristophanes suggests in his play *Frogs*, which was produced early in 405 B.C. (about six months after the battle of Arginusae). Among the things sailors know how to do, Aristophanes writes, is to "pass gas in a thalamian's face and foul his messmate with dung" (1074–1075). The same sort of thing is suggested by another passage in the play, in which the god Dionysus, made to row the ferryman Charon's boat across the Styx en route to the Underworld, complains about his discomfort (236–239):

> Dionysus: "I've got blisters, and my bottom's been oozing [or perhaps 'sweating'] for a while now. Pretty soon it will bend over [or 'peep out'] and let out a . . ."
> Chorus of frogs: "BREKEKEKEX KO-AX KO-AX!"

Dionysus is interrupted by the chorus of frogs, whose brekekekex ko-ax ko-ax—their croaked version of a rhythmic call meant to time the rowers' strokes—here stands in for the explosion Dionysus anticipates coming from his bowels. It's not clear to me whether the product of his oozing bottom is expected to be a gas or solid, but perhaps the passage is more effective for its ambiguity.

Aristophanes was writing comedy, of course, but the best comedy is usually reality-based. We know that fear has sometimes caused infantrymen—both ancient and modern[13]—to lose control of their bowels and bladders. Ancient naval warfare—oarsmen rowing blind to crash into another ship, not knowing when or whether they'd be rammed and boarded or speared and drowned themselves—was surely every bit as bowel-looseningly scary as marching

Figure 4. The three levels of rowers on the *Olympias*. From left to right: the thalamians, zygians, and thranites. © The Trireme Trust

toward the raised spears of an enemy phalanx. It was the particular misfortune of the thalamians that they would be nearest the fallout should their neighbors on the upper rowing benches suffer incontinence. As for flatulence, that was a problem the thalamians would have faced whatever the emotional state of their rowing mates.

For all the comfort of their position in the top tier, the thranites' job wasn't all sunshine and thyme-scented breezes. Rowing, often for many hours at a time, was physically demanding labor whatever a man's position on board, and the rowers will have suffered equally from aching backs and blisters and sore bottoms. (Each oarsman brought along his own cushion to sit on, by way of alleviating the last of these maladies.) The perks that the thranites enjoyed, moreover, came with a price. Their exposure to the open air meant they were at greater risk during battle from incoming missiles. Triremes were equipped with side screens that could somehow be hung from the deck to protect the thranites, but a passage from Thucydides suggests that they either weren't always used or weren't effective in all cases: during a battle in Syracuse's harbor in 413, Syracusans in small boats did a lot of damage by sailing up alongside Athenian ships and throwing javelins at the oarsmen.[14]

We know that thranites were sometimes paid more than other rowers. This may be partly because they faced greater risks in the exposed upper tier, but it is also likely that they were the most skilled members of the oar crew and could command higher wages for that reason. As the only rowers who could see their oars hitting the water, it was probably up to the thranites to communicate with the lower levels of rowers inboard of them, coaching them through difficulties when the rhythm of their stroke had been disrupted for some reason. This was the experience on the *Olympias*, where the thranites wound up serving as sort of team leaders of the triad of oarsman formed by themselves and the zygian and thalamian rowers alongside and below them.[15]

Maintaining a coordinated stroke while under oar was essential for the operation of a trireme. The experience of the *Olympias*, again, shows that one rower's mistake—easy enough to make with 170 oars slicing into the water so close to one another—could ripple through the ship, resulting in "instant and fast-spreading chaos." Keeping the oarsmen of the *Olympias* rowing in time required constant attention—coaching from the rowing master, an audible signal supplied by an onboard piper—and this while they were sailing in relatively calm waters, with no one trying to ram into the side of their ship. It would of course have been a far more difficult business for ancient rowers to maintain their rhythm in the chaos of battle, when failure to do so could prove lethal.[16]

For a trireme to perform well in such circumstances, its crew had to be well-trained. This was true, first, on an individual level. Oarsmen needed to be in good condition—accustomed specifically to the physical demands that rowing imposes—and they needed to know how to row a trireme in battle conditions. Men who made their living as oarsmen on triremes would have had no problems in this regard. But Athenians who did not regularly serve as rowers would have been ill-prepared if compelled to man the fleet in an emergency, even if they had experience of rowing in other contexts (e.g., on private boats used for travel). Even highly experienced, professional oarsmen, however, needed to be trained to work together as a team if they were to function effectively as a unit. For that reason fleets usually engaged in training exercises if fighting was expected: we hear of crews drilling for five or six or seven days before a battle, if they had the time. Unfortunately, as we'll see in the next chapter, circumstances didn't always permit a crew to train extensively before meeting the enemy.[17]

Battle Tactics

Athens' fleet, during its prime, was generally faster and more agile than any it fought, and the Athenians, who were constantly at sea perfecting their skills, excelled at offensive maneuvers that required speed for their performance. Our sources frequently refer to two of these maneuvers—the *diekplous* and the *periplous*—but without going into much detail: Thucydides tells us, for example, that the Athenians "relied particularly on their skilled use of the *diekplous* and *periplous*."[18] Precisely what each was is a matter of some dispute.

Diekplous literally means "a sailing through and out" and almost certainly refers to a ship (or ships) sailing through a gap between two vessels in an enemy's line of battle. (Normally a fleet formed for battle in "line abreast," that is, the triremes were lined up next to one another, usually in a single row, with their rams pointing toward the enemy's line.) Scholarly disagreement is focused on two issues: what the purpose of the *diekplous* was and how many ships were sailing through that one gap in the enemy line. Regarding the first point, some scholars maintain that, in performing a *diekplous*, a trireme was trying to cripple one of the ships it was moving past by sailing in close and breaking the enemy's oars against its own bow. This attack might then be followed by an attack on the ship's hull, the trireme that had broken through wheeling around to ram the disabled vessel near its stern. Neither Thucydides nor Herodotus refers to triremes shearing off the oars of enemy ships in battle, but a number of later sources describe the tactic. In particular, Diodorus, who wrote in the first century B.C., claims that Callicratidas, the Spartan navarch, broke the oars of a number of Athenian ships at Arginusae. Perhaps Diodorus's reference is anachronistic, but it seems possible, at least, that shearing off an enemy's oars was something fifth-century triremes might have been attempting during battle. That does not imply, however, and our late sources do not suggest, that an attack on the enemy's oars was the *purpose* of the *diekplous* or an intrinsic element of it, and I am not persuaded that it was. The more likely point of the *diekplous* was the second phase of the attack described above, for the ship performing the maneuver to get into a position behind the enemy's line from which it could, after a sharp turn, attack an enemy trireme in its vulnerable flank or stern (see fig. 5).[19]

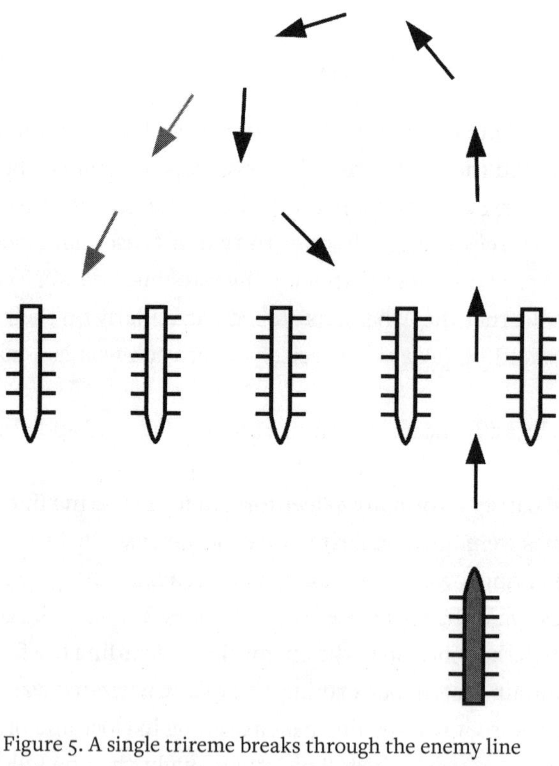

Figure 5. A single trireme breaks through the enemy line (*diekplous*) and wheels to attack a ship in its stern—possibly but not necessarily one of the ships next to which it broke through. © 2015 Debra Hamel

The second focus of debate concerns whether the *diekplous* was performed by a single ship or by a column of ships (i.e., ships in "line ahead"). On this point I agree with a number of scholars that triremes attempting to sail in column through a gap between ships in line abreast would leave themselves too vulnerable for the tactic to be practicable.[20] The ships under attack would not simply hold their position while the enemy attempted the *diekplous*: they would surely sail forward to ram the flanks of the vessels in line ahead. The *diekplous*, then, was more likely a maneuver performed by single ships, although it is possible that it was attempted simultaneously by a number of ships along the line.

We know of two defensive measures an ancient fleet could take to counter the *diekplous*. First, a fleet could deploy in two lines abreast instead of one, with the ships in the second line presumably stationed behind the gaps in the first. Any enemy ship attempting to break through the first line would be at risk of being rammed by ships in the second. A fleet could also defend against the *diekplous* by forming into a circular formation, or *kuklos*, hedgehog-like, with their sterns inward and their rams out (see fig. 6). The *kuklos* would certainly

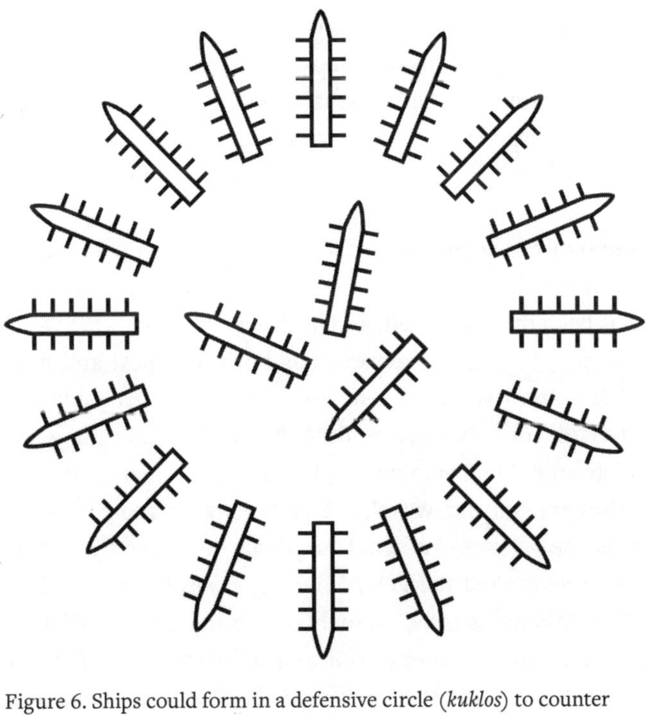

Figure 6. Ships could form in a defensive circle (*kuklos*) to counter the *diekplous*. © 2015 Debra Hamel

prevent any enemy ships from performing the *diekplous*, but it didn't make the ships so arranged invulnerable to attack. The *kuklos* was famously adopted by a Peloponnesian fleet during a battle that took place in the Corinthian Gulf in 429. The Peloponnesians' forty-seven ships formed into a circle—forty-two vessels forming the circumference with five ships in the center—to defend against an Athenian fleet of twenty ships. The Peloponnesians had the advantage in numbers, but their triremes were carrying extra troops and were thus no match for Athens' faster ships. The Athenians in turn formed in line ahead and sailed around the Peloponnesian circle, forcing it to contract by getting closer and closer and by feigning attacks. The idea was to get the Peloponnesian ships into so compressed a space that they would fall foul of each other. In addition, Phormio, the commander of the Athenian fleet, was waiting to give the signal to attack until a wind came up—as it regularly did at that time of day: the wind would stir the sea into a chop and make it difficult for the Peloponnesians (inferior sailors as they were) to navigate at all. In the end, everything happened as Phormio planned. The wind picked up and the Peloponnesian ships fell into confusion. Their oarsmen couldn't row properly. On deck they had to use poles to push their ships apart because they'd become clustered together. There was shouting and swearing and in the midst of all this, when the Peloponnesians were most vulnerable, the Athenians pounced. They disabled a number of enemy vessels on the spot, then captured twelve more that had managed to flee south toward the Peloponnese. Not a good day for the Peloponnesians, but they did succeed in defending their fleet against the *diekplous*, if nothing else.[21]

The second offensive measure mentioned by our sources is the *periplous*, which literally means "a sailing around." Like the *diekplous*, the nature of the *periplous* has been much debated, and in the end we can't know for sure what it was. It doesn't help that the word has both technical and nontechnical meanings. The Greek verb *periplein*, "to sail around," from which the noun *periplous* derives, could be used to describe any kind of sailing around: one would "sail around" the Peloponnese, for example, when making a trip from Athens to Corcyra, but that wasn't the same as performing the offensive tactic known as the *periplous*. When Thucydides describes the Athenian ships sailing in a circle around the Peloponnesian *kuklos* in 429, he uses the verb *periplein*. The Athenians were undoubtedly "sailing around" their enemy's fleet, but in doing so were they performing a technical *periplous*? Ian Whitehead argues in a 1987 paper that they were not, that this is not a technical use of the term, and I'm inclined to agree, primarily because indisputable references to the *periplous* in our sources don't suggest that it was a tactic adopted in response to a *kuklos*.[22]

Another possibility is that the *periplous* was an outflanking maneuver. If one fleet was longer than the other, it could sail around the end of the enemy's line and attack it from the rear. Fleets certainly did try to outflank one another. At Cynossema, for example, the Spartan fleet attempted to outflank the Athenians' right wing (which the Athenians countered by lengthening their line), but the verb Thucydides uses to describe the move is *hyperechein* ("to outflank"), not *periplein*.[23] Equating the *periplous* with an outflanking maneuver is an attractive solution, and it may be right—outflanking certainly would have involved "sailing around"—but as far as I know there isn't any solid evidence for the association.

H. T. Wallinga suggests that the *periplous* was a less definite activity than those suggested above. Instead, he writes, the term referred to ships "freely moving round in the open water between and behind opposing lines."[24] This general movement seems too vague an activity, however, for it to have had its own name, let alone for it to be paired with the *diekplous* in our sources as a skill at which the Athenians excelled.

A final possibility is suggested by Ian Whitehead. At 2.91–92, Thucydides describes a second battle that took place in the Corinthian Gulf in 429—Phormio's twenty triremes now pitted against a Peloponnesian fleet of seventy-seven ships. During the battle an Athenian ship that was being chased by an enemy trireme suddenly wheeled around a merchantman that was anchored in the harbor off Naupactus and rammed its pursuer amidships (see fig. 7). The verb Thucydides uses to describe the Athenian ship's turn is a participial form of *periplein*. For Whitehead, this *is* an instance of the verb being used in its technical sense. A *periplous*, in his view, was the act of turning sharply to attack an enemy to one's rear. It could be but was not necessarily preceded by a *diekplous*. (At 2.89.8, Thucydides mentions the *diekplous* in connection with a naval tactic called the *anastrophe*, which literally means "a turning about." The word seems to refer to the same sharp turn described above. For Whitehead, at any rate, the *anastrophe* and *periplous* are synonymous.) As I said above, we cannot identify the *periplous* with complete certainty, but I believe that Whitehead's explanation of the maneuver has the edge over competing theories.[25]

Speed was an asset in trireme warfare because ships needed to be able to accelerate and back water quickly and to make fast turns so as to outmaneuver the enemy. It doesn't follow, however, that triremes had to be rowed at top speed in order to ram an enemy ship. In fact, it appears that doing so could

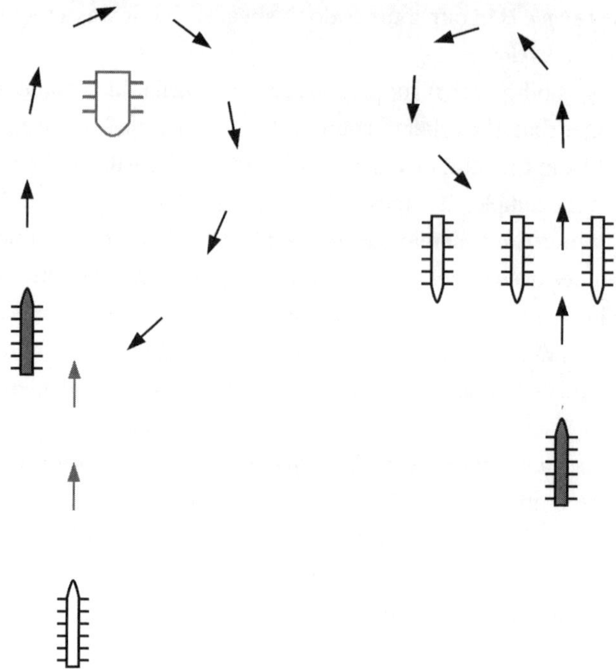

Figure 7. A trireme could wheel around to attack an enemy to its rear, either when fleeing from a pursuer *(left)* or after a *diekplous* *(right)*. Both may be examples of a *periplous*. © 2015 Debra Hamel

have been dangerous. At faster speeds the attacker's ram was more likely to become embedded in the hull of the vessel it struck (though this would also depend on the angle of attack). This was a problem because the attacking ship might then be boarded by any marines on the rammed ship who were still up to the task. Also, the ramming vessel would be unable to move and thus would be vulnerable to being rammed in turn by a third ship. Apart from the problem of getting one's ram stuck, an attack at high speed would increase the speed of the ramming vessel's deceleration, so its crew was more likely to be injured or even killed on impact. Rather than ramming at nine or ten knots, then—speeds that a fast vessel might achieve—triremes were likely rowing at much slower speeds when they rammed stationary ships or ships headed in their direction, perhaps only a few knots. A trireme that was chasing an enemy vessel, meanwhile, could inflict damage on its enemy's hull even if it was moving only half a knot faster than the pursued ship (e.g., nine and a half and nine knots, respectively).[26]

In order to perform the *diekplous* or the *periplous*, triremes needed not only speed but also sufficient room to maneuver in: it was no good trying to break through the enemy line if there wasn't enough space behind it in which to wheel around for an attack. The commander of a fleet could not always choose his battlefield, of course, but when he could, if he had fast ships, he would ordinarily want to fight in the open sea. The commander of a slower fleet, meanwhile, would want to fight in a confined space in order to neutralize to an extent his enemy's advantage in speed. Thucydides has Phormio describe his thinking on the issue in a harangue he is supposed to have delivered to his men before that second battle in the Gulf in 429, when the Athenians were outnumbered by a Peloponnesian fleet nearly four times the size of theirs. Phormio may or may not have said anything like this, but whatever the historicity of the speech, the tactical thinking in it is sound. Given his druthers, Phormio says, he will not fight the upcoming battle in the narrows: lack of space is a disadvantage when you have a small fleet of agile ships fighting against a larger but clumsier fleet. "The *diekplous* and *anastrophe*," Phormio says, "which are the tactics of better sailing vessels, are not possible in a small space. Instead the sea battle necessarily becomes a battle on land, and in *that* the larger fleet is stronger."[27]

There's a reason that triremes routinely carried at least a small cadre of hoplites. Sea battles could devolve into land battles, as Phormio calls them, if they were fought in a confined area, or if ships were unable to separate after one vessel had rammed another. In other words, if there wasn't enough room for a trireme to move around in, the ship could no longer be used as a weapon, a missile to be hurled against an enemy's hull. Instead, the trireme became a floating platform on which men fought what amounted to a land battle on deck. This could even be the preferred tactic of a fleet—if it was slower or had extra men on board—in which case, grappling hooks (literally "iron hands" in Greek) could be used to reel in an enemy ship or keep it from getting away. Thucydides pooh-poohs fighting on deck as old fashioned in his account of a battle fought off Corcyra in 433: it didn't take nautical skill, after all, for men to stab at one another with swords on board a ship. But even the Athenians, skilled sailors that they were, could be compelled to forego their fancy tactics and fight a land battle at sea. In the final battle in the harbor of Syracuse in 413, the Athenians' ships were structurally weaker than those of the enemy (because the Syracusans had reinforced their prows to survive bow-to-bow collisions). The battle, moreover, took place in a very tight space—"the most ships fought on this occasion in the narrowest area ever," Thucydides tells us. The Athenians' only hope was to pack grappling irons and extra men on board and fight the Syracusans on deck. The battle was a massive and confusing affair—nearly two hundred ships in a sea churned by oars, ramming and being rammed at once or simply colliding for want of room, javelins and arrows and stones flying and marines lunging deck to deck as the Athenians tried to save themselves. In the end they were defeated at sea, then chased and hounded overland, captured and killed or left to die of deprivation, scarcely a man among them surviving to see Athens again. Technical expertise meant little, unfortunately, if there wasn't enough sea room to use it in.[28]

Death at Sea

Ramming was a dangerous business not only for the rammed but potentially for the rammer as well. Crew members of either ship could be injured or killed by the force of the collision. Thalamians sitting near the point of impact in the rammed ship were particularly vulnerable to injury from splintering wood and the ram itself. If the attacking ship was unable to extricate itself from the ship it had struck, meanwhile, the marines and archers on either deck got busy trying to clear the enemy's vessel of armed defenders. They might then board the enemy ship and begin killing oarsmen, who were unarmed and, given the conditions in which they were working, probably almost naked. Swords and arrows and spears, then, javelins and even rocks could wound or kill sailors in battle, either when the fight had devolved into a land battle at sea or beforehand, when archers and stone throwers took aim from nearby vessels.

If a ship was rammed, it filled with water and floated half submerged, which meant that survivors could cling to the wreckage for some time. But first they had to get out of the ship. The Hellenic Navy was able to perform a total evacuation over the side of the modern trireme *Olympias* in only twenty-four seconds, but these modern sailors didn't perform the exercise while their ship was sinking. When a trireme was rammed, some of its oarsmen would likely have drowned before they could clamber out of the hull, particularly the thalamians, and particularly if they were injured. Survivors who did make it out might still be killed by the enemy while clinging to their ship's wreckage. After the battle off Corcyra in 433, the victorious Corinthians sailed around through the flotsam killing survivors—sometimes even mistakenly killing their own men in their thirst for blood. Aeschylus, too, seems to be describing just this sort of slaughter of men clinging to wreckage in his play *Persians* when he writes that the Greeks at Salamis "went on beating the Persians, slicing them up, with fragments of oar and bits of wreckage, like tuna or some catch of fish" (424–426).[29]

Naval battles were usually fought within a few thousand yards of land. Some survivors might try to save themselves after their ship had been rammed by swimming to shore, but in that case, of course, they ran the risk of drowning or being killed by the enemy en route. If the coast wasn't held by friendly forces, moreover, sailors might be captured or butchered by the enemy once they managed to crawl ashore. If one is ranking deaths by their desirability, this is surely among the most cruel—to have survived your ship's ramming and safely dodged missile fire, arrows plinking into the water around you, only to be finished off the moment you reach dry land.[30]

As the above litany surely makes clear, there were a great many ways that a trireme's crewmen could die at sea. In our next chapter we'll see what manner of death met those unfortunates who gave their all at Arginusae.

-III-

The Battle of Arginusae: From Manning the Fleet to Collecting Corpses

In engagements of 200 to 300 ships . . . 40,000 to 60,000 men, the equivalent of a large Greek city, were at once hurling missiles, rowing, boarding, clinging to wreckage, and swimming to shore. So in minutes the seas were flooded with the flotsam and jetsam of broken triremes, bodies, and men splashing and clinging to debris.

Victor Hanson, *A War Like No Other*

WHEN THE TRIREME that had slipped through the blockade at Mytilene arrived in Athens, it prompted a firestorm of activity. Our sources provide only the briefest accounts of what happened next, spare references to numbers of ships readied and men enrolled for service. But Aristophanes, in a comedy performed nearly twenty years earlier, describes in a breathless string of phrases the sights and sounds of a city preparing a fleet for war:

> The polis would be full of the ruckus of soldiers, of shouting around the ship's captain, wages paid, figureheads of Athena gilded, the roaring colonnade, rations measured, wineskins, oar loops, haggling over jars, garlic, olives, nets of onions, garlands, anchovies, flute girls, black eyes; and the dockyard full of oars being planed, pegs hammered, the thalamian oar ports fitted with sleeves, flutes, rowing masters, whistles, pipes. (*Acharnians*, lines 545–554)

We may imagine that the Athenians were similarly occupied once they resolved to send aid to their fleet in Mytilene, the glory that was Greek warfare preceded by the less rarified business of real life—carpentry, prostitutes, fist fights, grocery shopping.

The Scratch Fleet

The Athenians wasted no time in responding to the news from Mytilene. They voted at once to send out a fleet, and they were able to man and launch it within thirty days. There is some dispute in our sources about the number of ships they dispatched. Xenophon tells us they launched 110 triremes and that these were supplemented by more than 40 ships from Athens' allies as well as by any Athenian ships that happened to be abroad. In the end, he reports, the fleet that soon collected at Samos numbered somewhat more than 150 vessels. According to Diodorus, however, the Athenians launched only 60 ships, and these were supplemented by 90 allied vessels, for a total of 150. Both accounts are problematic. It's hard to believe, for one thing, that Athens' allies could scrape together 90 triremes among them. And neither author's enumeration accounts for the 30-odd ships the Athenians should still have had at Samos. (Conon and his colleagues, remember, had only manned 70 ships out of a fleet of more than 100 before they sailed from Samos to Lesbos.) Both authors are agreed, at any rate, that the Athenians ultimately put together a fleet of about 150 ships. However many of these were launched from Athens, it's clear that the Athenians must already have been preparing a fleet for some time when the news came from Mytilene: they can't have constructed 60 or more ships from scratch in the space of only thirty days.[1]

If Xenophon is right about the number of ships that were launched, the Athenians would have needed a crew of 22,000 to man them, 18,700 of them rowers. (A fleet of sixty ships, on the other hand, would have required a crew of 12,000, including 10,200 rowers.) Our sources suggest that the Athenians went to extraordinary lengths to enroll enough men for service. Xenophon tells us they "put on board all those who were of military age, both slave and free" and adds that "many of the *hippeis* also went on board." *Hippeis*, or "knights," were members of the second highest economic class in Athens and as such normally served in Athens' cavalry. It's not clear from Xenophon whether the *hippeis* were required to serve in the new fleet as rowers or marines, but either assignment would have been unusual for them. Xenophon may be exaggerating when he says that "all" who were of military age were required to serve, but the fact that *hippeis* were enrolled suggests that the Athenians were indeed tapping unusual sources to fill their quotas.[2]

Xenophon's reference to the enrollment of slaves may likewise surprise readers, but recruiting slaves for service in the fleet was not in itself unusual. Our evidence suggests that slaves served regularly alongside free oarsmen, who might be Athenian citizens, foreigners who were residents of Athens, manumitted slaves, or foreign mercenaries. Indeed, it appears that slaves and their masters often served together as oarsmen in the same fleet, when possible on the same ship; that way, slaves could earn money for their owners while remaining under their close supervision. (If they did row together we may assume that the slave was the more likely of the two to end up among the unfortunate thalamians.) What *was* unusual about the Athenians' enrollment of slaves on this occasion is something Xenophon doesn't mention. At lines 693–694 of Aristophanes' *Frogs*, the chorus of the play refers to "those who fought in a single naval battle becoming Plataeans and masters rather than slaves." A scholiast (ancient commentator) on the passage explains the remark, citing the fifth-century historian Hellanicus of Lesbos: "Hellanicus says that the slaves who fought with them in the naval battle were freed and that, enrolled as Plataeans, they shared political rights with them [the Athenians]." The Plataeans were staunch, longtime allies of Athens—the only ones who had stood with the Athenians against the Persians at the Battle of Marathon in 490. After the Spartans destroyed Plataea in 427, the Athenians granted citizenship to the 212 Plataeans who had escaped to Athens—an extraordinary gesture, given that historically the Athenians were jealous guardians of the privileges of citizenship. Now, Aristophanes tells us, the Athenians offered this same reward to the slaves who were enrolled for service in the fleet: if they survived the fight to come, the slaves would return to Athens as free men and citizens, members of a community in which they enjoyed the same political rights as their former masters.[3]

Although he does not mention the slaves' enfranchisement, Xenophon hints at a possible explanation for it when he tells us that the Athenians enrolled in the fleet "all those who were of military age, both slave and free." This, in other words, was a general call-up of all fit slaves, which suggests that there would probably have been a larger percentage of slaves than usual serving in the fleet and also a larger percentage who would be serving unsupervised, without their masters present: not all the slaves' owners would have been fit for service themselves. Add to this that the Spartans had been trying to lure rowers away from Athens' fleet by offering higher wages and it made good sense for the Athenians to try to guarantee their slaves' loyalty by offering them freedom and enfranchisement. The slaves would be less likely to desert to the Spartans if they were guaranteed citizenship in the polis they were fighting for.

Diodorus doesn't say anything about the enrollment of slaves in 406, but he does claim that the Athenians offered citizenship to any foreigners or metics (these could be foreign residents of Athens or manumitted slaves) who fought with them. One might object to this that the metics, who were obliged to serve in Athens' military anyway, should not have required an incentive to do so. But rewarding the slaves so generously while doing nothing for any metics who signed up—indeed, elevating the slaves to a higher status than that of the metics—could only have led to resentment among the latter group. Enfranchising the metics, then, was politic: it wasn't in the Athenians' interest to alienate a significant portion of their crew.[4]

In the last chapter we emphasized the importance of training for a trireme's crew. For a ship to perform well the oarsmen manning it needed to be accustomed to the physical demands of rowing, and the crew as a whole needed to be trained to work together as a cohesive unit. The scratch crews that rowed off from Athens in the summer of 406 to rescue Conon's fleet in Mytilene were lacking in both respects. Granted, some experienced rowers must have been among the ten or eighteen thousand oarsmen who were called upon to man the fleet. But a large percentage of those thousands had very little or no experience as rowers in a trireme: metic tradesman who were buying their citizenship with a stint on the rowing benches, slaves whose masters ordinarily set them tasks other than service in the fleet, middle-class Athenians who normally served as infantrymen, aristocrats who were more accustomed to life on horseback than on a trireme's lurching deck. Needless to say, these inexperienced crews had never sailed together before, never practiced the tactics that generations of Athenian seamen had used to dominate their adversaries. All the practice these crews would get was on the journey they now made to Samos, some 175 nautical miles to the east.

Battle Formations

When the Spartan navarch Callicratidas heard that the Athenians had arrived at Samos with a relief force, he sailed off to meet them with 120 ships, leaving 50 behind under the command of Eteonicus to maintain the blockade of Mytilene. We can't know what Callicratidas was thinking, but Donald Kagan is right to point out that waiting until the Athenians brought the fight to Mytilene's harbor was a bad idea: the Spartans would then have to face Athens' new fleet to the front while Conon's 38 ships threatened from the rear. Hoping to avoid this, perhaps, Callicratidas sailed south, stopping for the night at

Cape Malea, the southeastern-most point of Lesbos. The Athenians, meanwhile, had sailed north, and wound up spending the night on one of the Arginusae Islands, which lay only about nine miles to the east of the Spartans' position. Xenophon tells us that the Spartans could in fact see the Athenians' fires that night from Lesbos. One can almost picture the scene—wine-dark sea and ink-black sky broken near the horizon by flames, the enemy almost touchable across the water. Callicratidas toyed with the idea of sailing east around midnight to surprise the Athenians in their sleep, but a storm came on—heavy rain and lightning—and prevented it: launching the fleet in weather like that could have been disastrous. The Spartans sailed out at dawn instead to face an enemy that was wide awake and fully prepared to meet them.[5]

The Athenian fleet of 150 ships was under the command of eight generals at Arginusae. Three of the ten men who had originally been elected to the generalship for the year were not present. Conon was trapped in Mytilene. Leon, whose ship had been captured after it slipped through the Spartan blockade of Mytilene, was either dead or in Spartan custody. And Archestratus was assuredly dead. The Athenians had sent out a man named Lysias to serve as his replacement. Each of the eight generals at Arginusae commanded a squadron of 15 ships in the battle to come. There were four of these squadrons on either wing of the Athenians' formation, the ships drawn up in line abreast in two rows of 30 vessels each. Aristocrates and Diomedon commanded the forward squadrons on the Athenians' left wing, with Pericles and Erasinides behind them. And Protomachus and Thrasyllus were on the right, backed by Lysias and Aristogenes.[6] The language Xenophon uses in describing the Athenian center has led to some controversy regarding the arrangement of ships there. He tells us that a squadron of ten Samian vessels was next to Diomedon, drawn up in a single line. Next to them were the ten ships of the Athenian taxiarchs (military officers), which were also in a single line. So much is clear. But Xenophon goes on to mention a third squadron of ships made up of the three ships of the navarchs (Athenian naval officers) and some number of allied vessels. This squadron was stationed *epi de tautais*, Xenophon says. This would normally mean "behind them," that is, behind the ships of the taxiarchs and Samians. The problem is that if the phrase means "behind them" here it appears to contradict Xenophon's claim that the other two squadrons in the center were in single lines. Donald Kagan has argued that *epi de tautais* should instead be understood to mean "in addition to these." The third squadron, by this understanding, could have been next to rather than behind the other vessels in the center. This would get rid of Xenophon's contradiction, but it is a less natural interpretation of the Greek. Based on Xenophon's language alone, then, the choice between these two problematic options is a toss-up. We need to consider other factors before we come to a decision about the Athenian center.[7]

Diodorus, our other source for the Athenian formation at Arginusae, is for the most part unhelpful. He claims that Pericles was on the right wing, but he later has him fighting on the left. He puts Thrasyllus on the right as well but doesn't specify the positions of the other generals (they were stationed "along the entire line"), and he says nothing about their individual squadrons. But Diodorus does provide one important piece of information that does not appear in Xenophon's account. He says that in order to make their battle line as long as possible, the Athenians included the Arginusae Islands in their formation. We'll discuss precisely what this means below. For now, we need to consider whether the information is at all credible.

Vivienne Gray argues that Diodous's information should be rejected as unhistorical. Diodorus, she explains, tends to try to amplify the importance of the conflicts he's describing. For example, he claims that on the day after Conon and the Athenians had lost thirty ships to the Spartans at Mytilene, they fought a second battle—and a fearsome one, judging from his description of it. Xenophon, however, says nothing about this second battle, and it is likely to be pure fiction: two battles in the harbor of Mytilene make for a better story than one. In Gray's view, Diodorus's report that the Athenians included the islands in their formation is a similar invention. As we'll see, the formation they adopted compelled the Spartans to divide their own line in two. The result was that there were in effect four fleets fighting at Arginusae, the two parts of the Spartan line fighting separately against different sections of the Athenians' formation. Diodorus claims that this novelty, and the sheer number of ships engaged in the fight, amazed onlookers. And that, for Gray, was the point: Diodorus made up the detail about the island in order to make the battle seem even more impressive than it was.

I am inclined to disagree with Gray's analysis, however, and to accept Diodorus's evidence. The inclusion of the islands in the Athenian line seems to me too unconventional a detail to be dismissed as obviously unhistorical. It's one thing to double a battle by inserting a conventional description of a second fight into one's text. Doubling a battle by inserting a land mass into one of the combatants' battle lines strikes me as a far less likely invention. Moreover, the battle formation that the Athenians adopted—if Diodorus's information is accepted and interpreted as suggested below—was brilliant, and it goes some way toward explaining how Athens' ragtag fleet of landlubbers managed to defeat the Spartans' more experienced sailors.[8]

The Arginusae are a cluster of three small islands east of Lesbos, just off the coast of Asia Minor. The two main islands lie next to each other—modern Garipadasi to the west and Kalemadasi to the east—running longer north to south than they are wide. The third island is a speck of land north of Garipadasi. There are two theories about how the islands could have been incorporated into the Athenian line: either they were a genuine interruption in the Athenians' battle order, so that some of their ships were to the north of Garipadasi and some to the south, or the Athenians' wings were on either side of the island and their center was posted in front of it.[9]

Diodorus doesn't tell us how the Athenians included the islands in their formation, but as we've seen he does say that the purpose of their doing so was to make their line as long as possible. If the thirty ships in the Athenian center were positioned in a single line abreast in front of the island, as some scholars suggest, they would have taken up about six hundred yards of sea. (This is assuming a frontage of roughly twenty yards per ship.) Garipadasi is roughly 1300 yards long now (though admittedly its dimensions may have changed over the last 2500 years). Posting their center in front of Garipadasi would therefore have effectively lengthened the Athenians' line by about seven hundred yards (the length of the island less the length of the Athenian center). If the Athenians stationed their center next to the island, however, their line would have been longer yet, by six hundred yards if the ships were posted in a single line abreast, and by perhaps nine hundred yards if they were in two lines. (Ships stationed in two lines abreast could probably be spaced more widely apart than ships in a single line: a reasonable estimate is forty-five yards of frontage per ship. The Athenian center, drawn up in two lines abreast with twenty ships in the first line, would have taken up nine hundred yards of sea.) If the Athenians wanted to increase the length of their line as much as possible, as Diodorus claims, stationing their center alongside the island rather than in front of it and in two lines abreast was clearly the more desirable option. This, I suggest, is the formation the Athenians adopted.[10]

If the Athenian center was posted in two lines abreast, it follows that Xenophon's *epi de tautais* should be translated as "behind them" rather than "in addition to them." We are still left with the problem of Xenophon contradicting himself, since he claims that the first two squadrons in the Athenian center were in single lines. But as we've seen, his language is problematic whether we understand him to mean that the third squadron was "behind" those other ships or "in addition to" them.

It remains to consider whether the Athenian center was posted to the north or south of the island. Three considerations suggest it was to the south. First, the right wing, taking up some 1350 yards, would have fit very nicely between the island and the mainland where it bulges west into the Aegean (see map 4). Second, when Xenophon describes the Athenians' battle order, he uses spatial expressions to describe the positions of the squadrons relative to one another. Aristocrates was on the far left, and Diomedon was next to him (*meta de tauta*). Pericles and Erasinides were behind them (*epetetakto*). The Samians were next to Diomedon (*para*). Then came the taxiarchs (*exomenai*). And the third squadron in the center was behind them (*epi de tautais*). Protomachus, Xenophon next tells us, held the right wing, and Thrasyllus was next to him (*para*), with Lysias and Aristogenes behind them (*epetetakto*). Note that the positions of the squadrons on the right wing are not given with reference to the Athenian center. If there was an interruption in the Athenian line, Xenophon's language implies that it was between the center and the right wing. Finally, with the center south of the island, the Athenians' left wing would have stretched farther out to sea by nine hundred yards. The longer line is more in keeping with Xenophon's comment that the Athenians' extended their left wing out to sea.[11]

The Athenians had more ships than the Spartans at Arginusae—150 against 120—but they were less skilled sailors than their enemy and they knew it. They therefore adopted a formation that was intended, Xenophon tells us, to protect them from the Spartan *diekplous*. Their entire fleet—both their wings and, as I've argued above, their center—was arranged in two lines abreast to prevent the Spartans from performing the maneuver. But the formation the Athenians adopted did more than protect them from the *diekplous*. To the south of Garipadasi, the northern flank of the Athenians' center was likely adjacent to the island and therefore protected from being outflanked at that point. The Athenians' right wing, meanwhile, was posted adjacent to land on both flanks, protected to the south by the island and to the north by a promontory that juts into the sea from the mainland. If the Athenian right held its position, it could not be outflanked on either wing. Meanwhile, if any Spartan ships managed to break through the Athenian line on either side of Garipadasi, they could not follow up a victory there by sailing behind the islands to attack the other flank from the rear. Godfrey Hutchinson points out that the channels between the two islands and between Kalemadasi and the mainland are nowadays too shallow to be navigable. They likely were in antiquity as well.[12]

The Athenians had thus adopted a very strong defensive position, but their formation brought offensive advantages as well. Including the island in their line made for a much longer array than the Athenians would have had otherwise, 4900 yards total (about 2.75 miles). In particular, 90 Athenian ships extended south or southwest from Garipadasi for some 2250 yards (1.25 miles). The Spartans, meanwhile, had arranged their 120 ships in a single line abreast—prepared, Xenophon tells us, to perform the *diekplous* and the *periplous*. If each of their ships took up twenty yards of sea, their entire line would have extended for only 2400 yards. Diodorus tells us that Callicratidas divided his fleet in two because he couldn't make it equal to the Athenians'. (Callicratidas commanded the segment of the fleet that was on the right, and the Spartan left was under the command of the Theban Thrasondas.) Diodorus doesn't tell us how many ships were in each section of the divided fleet, but I would assume, absent other evidence, that Callicratidas arranged things so that the segments were roughly proportionate in number to the Athenians' numbers on either side of the island, thus about 72 ships on the Spartan right and 48 on the left. But however the Spartan fleet was arranged, the Athenians had the advantage in length: the Spartans could be outflanked. Moreover, because Callicratidas had divided his fleet, the Spartans now had four flanks that were vulnerable to attack.[13]

To sum things up, the Athenians who fought at Arginusae were less experienced sailors than the Spartans, but they had more ships than the enemy, and their position was stronger, both offensively and defensively. We'll see below how this combination of advantages and disadvantages played out for them in the heat of battle.

The Battle

Neither Xenophon nor Diodorus has much to tell us about the actual fighting at Arginusae. Indeed, Xenophon tells the whole story of the battle in three sentences. Diodorus's account is longer and more detailed than Xenophon's, but it is also more generic and is mostly concerned with the alleged heroics of the Spartan navarch Callicratidas. Having learned from a seer prior to the battle that he was destined to die, Diodorus writes, Callicratidas aimed to go out in a blaze of glory. He was ramming ships left and right, cutting a swath through the Athenian line, when finally he rammed the Athenian general Pericles' trireme with unusual violence and got stuck: the Spartans couldn't extract their ram from the ship they'd holed. Now the Athenian victims became the aggressors. They used a grappling hook to keep the Spartans immobile, then boarded

Callicratidas's trireme and killed everyone on it. Callicratidas himself fought brilliantly and held out for a long time, but he was finally overwhelmed by the sheer numbers against him, and he went down in whatever the pre-gunpowder equivalent of a hail of bullets was—a flurry of sword thrusts, I suppose. Using a hackneyed expression to describe Callicratidas's end, as it's told by Diodorus, seems apt, as it's hard to take this formulaic account of a heroic death seriously. I find Xenophon's brief mention of Callicratidas's death far more credible, principally because his version lacks the made-for-Hollywood glamour of Diodorus's account. According to Xenophon, Callicratidas fell overboard when his ship rammed an enemy trireme, and he disappeared. It's a prosaic but believable way to go: simply managing to stay on one's ship while it was ramming or being rammed must have been a real problem for the crew members who were stationed on a trireme's deck during battle.[14]

Apart from the fact that Callicratidas died, we know very little about what happened at Arginusae. Xenophon tells us that the battle lasted for a long time and that while it was initially fought in close order, the ships later were scattered. This is what we would expect, that as the fighting wore on and the sea filled with wrecks, the combatants eventually lost their formation. We know that the Spartan line collapsed sometime after Callicratidas's death and that the Spartans fled south toward Phocaea and Cyme on the mainland and southwest toward Chios. Xenophon and Diodorus disagree, however, on what preceded their retreat. According to Xenophon, the Spartans were first defeated on their left wing. But Diodorus says the Spartan right fled first, and the Athenians who routed them then turned against the Spartan left. After the Spartans took to flight, the Athenians pursued them for some time, according to Diodorus, filling the sea with wreckage and corpses as they did so, but Xenophon tells us nothing about the pursuit. Finally, we know that twenty-five Athenian ships were disabled in the battle, but the ships of the taxiarchs, navarchs, and Samians were not among them. The Spartans, on the other hand, lost at least seventy triremes—more than sixty allied vessels, and nine of the ten ships the Spartans themselves had contributed to the fleet. These had presumably been stationed on the Spartans' right wing with Callicratidas.[15]

So much we know. Forming a coherent narrative from this minimal information would be a matter of guesswork. We can paint the picture only in broad strokes. Their formation, as we have understood it, would suggest that the Athenians were probably more aggressive on their left wing than on the right. Their left stretched far out to sea and could arc around the Spartan right to outflank it and attack from the rear. This would be consistent with the high losses reported for the Spartan ships positioned on the right—nine of ten disabled in the fight. On the Athenians' right wing, where they had a strong defensive position—both of their flanks anchored to land—they may have been less aggressive, holding their own against the Spartan left and keeping that segment of the enemy fleet occupied until their own left could come up in support—precisely what Diodorus describes as happening in the fight. Contingents from the Athenian center, south of the island, could also have attacked the exposed internal flank of the Spartan right—though if they did so they managed it without suffering significant losses. Throughout their line, both north and south of the island, the Athenians' second row of ships would have been well placed to ram any Spartan triremes attempting the *diekplous*. As Godfrey Hutchinson points out, the Athenians could also have effectively countered prow-to-prow attacks. If the Spartans attempted to ram ships in the Athenians' front line head-on—relying on reinforced prows to survive the collision as the Syracusans had done in 413—the targeted Athenian ships could grapple their attackers, making them vulnerable to ramming by ships in the Athenians' second line. Once a ship was grappled, of course, it changed from a floating missile into a platform for fighting on deck—the sea battle morphing into a battle on land, with all the chaos and carnage that entailed: marines stabbing with spears, limbs severed and slashed by thrusting swords, black blood pulsing onto the decks, the ring of iron on iron. This, we can imagine, is the sort of scene that played itself out all along the line at Arginusae when the fighting got close.[16]

Our sources don't explain why the Athenians triumphed at Arginusae despite the inexperience of their crews, and the question has puzzled historians. We'll never know exactly what happened during the battle, of course, but surely the size of the Athenians' fleet and the formation they adopted were both important factors in their victory. Someone on Team Athens was a smart enough tactician to recognize the potential benefits of their location, and the Athenians had enough ships to make the battlefield work for them. In the thick of the fighting, moreover, those extra thirty ships the Athenians had may well have been decisive.

The Athenians thus overcame their technical deficiencies with numbers and the smart prepositioning of their ships. Whatever they did during the battle, they managed not to undermine these initial advantages. And once they had forced the Spartans to flee, the battle was won. The Spartans may in fact have suffered the majority of their losses during this final phase of the battle, when their ships, out of formation and rowing frenziedly to the south, were particularly vulnerable to attack. Although Xenophon doesn't mention the Athenians' pursuit, it's likely enough that they chased the Spartans for some distance at least—perhaps four or five miles, though this is little more than a guess—before they returned to the islands.[17]

Once they got back to Arginusae, the Athenians needed to wrap things up the way sailors always did after a battle: by rescuing, capturing, or killing, as appropriate, any of the men they found still alive in the water, by collecting their dead and towing in any salvageable wrecks, and by putting up a trophy on some nearby piece of land to commemorate their victory at sea. Something had yet to be done, moreover, about the thirty-eight ships that were still trapped in Mytilene, and the sooner the better.

Rescue and Recovery

Diodorus writes that the coastline of Asia Minor near Cyme and Phocaea was strewn with corpses and wreckage after the battle, and we can well believe it. The Spartans and their allies lost at a minimum seventy ships in the fight, and few of the men who were aboard them would have survived: the Spartans, in desperate flight and separated from one another, were not in a position to mount a timely rescue operation. After the battle, then, some fourteen thousand enemy bodies—living, for the time being, and dead—were bobbing in the water south of Arginusae or sinking beneath it, slumped over wreckage or imprisoned in the submerged hulls of the triremes they had rowed and been unable to escape. Eventually the corpses that sank would resurface and be washed ashore to dot the beaches and rot in the sun if no one found them, bloated and blackened. The lucky ones would be discovered and buried by friends or scrupulous locals.[18]

The Athenians had men in the water too, of course, both living and dead. Presumably these were concentrated closer to the Arginusae Islands, where the battle had been fought, as the victors were unlikely to have suffered many casualties themselves during the pursuit. The Athenians would want, ideally, to get to their wrecks as soon as possible after the battle, certainly within a few hours. Obviously speed was essential for rescuing the survivors, but the Athenians would also want to collect as many bodies as they could before they began to sink. There was no guarantee that the Athenians would find their dead once they'd slipped beneath the waves: in a day or two or three, after the corpses had resurfaced or washed to shore, the Athenian fleet might not be anywhere near Arginusae. Besides, the ugly business of retrieving the dead would only become uglier the longer they waited. Once carted back to shore the bodies would be identified, if possible, and cremated, and the ashes stored so they could be returned to Athens for burial.

It was not always possible to recover the corpses of all those who had been killed in battle, particularly if they'd died at sea, but retrieving the bodies they could find would have been a priority for the Athenians. It was important to the Greeks generally that corpses—even the bodies of strangers—be provided with a proper burial. Indeed, the Athenians reportedly had a law that bid "anyone who happens upon an unburied corpse to throw earth upon it." The men in the water weren't strangers, of course: most of the Athenians who made it through the battle intact likely knew someone who hadn't. Bringing home the remains of those who had died at Arginusae would thus have mattered to the Athenians on a personal level. Rescuing the survivors and retrieving the dead, then, were both high-priority tasks.[19]

The Athenians had lost twenty-five ships, which means that some five thousand of their men were in the water after the battle. This is a rough estimate. Add to those five thousand any of the crew on undamaged ships who had been wounded or killed in the fighting and gone overboard. Subtract any survivors who had made their way to shore—which wasn't unlikely if any of the disabled vessels had been rammed near Garipadasi. Roughly five thousand bodies, then, but it is impossible to know how many of them were already dead by the time the Athenians returned to Arginusae after the battle and pursuit, and how many were still alive. Scholarly estimates range from "more than a thousand" survivors to twenty-five hundred, but the number could have been higher yet. That said, it's probably safe to assume that there were at least a thousand men awaiting rescue, a larger than usual percentage of them Athenian citizens, and many of them men for whom Arginusae was their first experience of trireme warfare. Having played their part in Athens' unexpected victory, they now clung to the hulls of their half-submerged vessels, asking one another how long it might take for the rescue ships to get there. Meanwhile, the cool waters of the Aegean were slowly sapping their bodies of heat.[20]

After they had pursued the fleeing Spartans for some distance, the Athenians returned to Arginusae to regroup. George Grote has criticized them for taking the time to convene at the islands rather than immediately rescuing their survivors, but meeting at Arginusae first made sense. Gathering the fleet in one place would allow the Athenians to see how many of their ships were unaccounted for and thus roughly how many men needed saving. The generals could use this information to mount an organized rescue operation, assigning an adequate number of ships to the tasks of rescuing the men and towing in salvageable wrecks. Beyond that, the Athenians' tactical situation made a meeting of the Athenian command especially important. The Athenians had to get to their wrecks as soon as possible, but they also needed to do something about the blockade at Mytilene. The Spartans still had 50 ships at Lesbos under the command of Eteonicus. If this fleet managed to join up with the Spartan ships that had fled south after Arginusae, the Athenians would again have to face a formidable enemy fleet not much smaller than theirs—more than 90 Spartan ships against their own one 125. It would be much easier to deal with the different contingents of the Spartan fleet separately.

The generals at Arginusae reportedly debated which task they should undertake, Erasinides urging that they go in full force to Mytilene, while Diomedon said they should all sail out and attend to the wrecks and the shipwrecked. Thrasyllus suggested a compromise: the generals could sail against Eteonicus with part of the fleet while leaving some ships behind at Arginusae to sail to the wrecks and rescue any survivors. Forty-seven ships were tasked with the latter chore—three from each of the generals' squadrons plus the ships of the navarchs, Samians, and taxiarchs. These rescue ships would be under the command of two of the trierarchs, Theramenes and Thrasybulus, and some of the taxiarchs. The rescue operation would be in good hands: Theramenes and Thrasybulus, the generals would later explain, were competent officers and had previously served as generals themselves.[21]

Unfortunately, Thrasyllus's sensible suggestion ultimately came to nothing. "Wind and a great storm" came up and prevented the Athenians from accomplishing either task. Forced to ride out the weather at Arginusae, they made camp and set up a trophy to commemorate their victory. (This was probably either an enemy trireme or the wooden statue affixed above its ram, pulled onto the beach and dedicated to Poseidon.) Diodorus suggests that the ships' crews were to blame for the Athenians' failure to sail: "They opposed picking up the corpses because of the hardships they'd endured in the battle and the size of the waves," he writes. One can easily read into this statement the idea that the crews were derelict out of cowardice. Certainly Grote assumed as much. Writing in the mid-nineteenth century, he contrasted the Athenians' behavior disapprovingly with that of the English navy, whose officers and men would probably volunteer for service in like circumstances, "against the most desperate risks, in a cause so profoundly moving all their best sympathies." Maybe so. But nineteenth-century English sailors weren't putting to sea in fragile wooden ships whose hulls were perforated by oar holes mere feet above the waterline: triremes, as we said above, didn't fare well in bad weather. Naturally, our sources can't describe the storm to us in modern meteorological terms—winds measuring such and such on the Beaufort scale—but strong winds, sometimes blowing at gale force (the so-called Etesian, or annual winds), are not uncommon in the Aegean during the summer. And as we've seen, a storm had also occurred the night before the battle, which suggests that the area was experiencing a patch of bad weather. We can well believe that the storm that prompted the Athenians to remain at Arginusae was legitimately severe enough to warrant their delay.[22]

Sometime after the battle Eteonicus received news of the Spartans' defeat and pulled out of Mytilene, presumably anxious to avoid the situation we imagined earlier—his fifty ships sandwiched between Conon's thirty-eight and the victorious Athenian fleet. Conon, after being trapped in Mytilene for more than a month, was now finally free to leave. He sailed east toward Arginusae after the storm had passed and met up with the Athenians, who were on their way to rescue him—too late to do anything about Eteonicus. Neither of our sources has much to tell us about what the Athenian fleet, now reunited, got up to next. Xenophon writes simply, "The Athenians put in at Mytilene, and from there they sailed against Chios, and after accomplishing nothing there they sailed off to Samos." Diodorus adds that the Athenians used Samos as a base from which they laid waste enemy territory. Both authors then turn their attention abruptly to what happened when news of the battle and its aftermath reached Athens.[23]

Before we follow Xenophon and Diodorus to Athens, however, we need to backtrack and consider what happened to those five thousand bodies we left bobbing in the waters around Arginusae. Our sources suggest that nothing whatsoever was done about them. Neither Xenophon nor Diodorus says anything about the Athenians attempting to rescue or retrieve them once the storm had abated. Diodorus, moreover, repeatedly claims that the Athenian commanders at Arginusae allowed the men who died in the battle to go unburied, which suggests that they blithely sailed off after the storm without a backward glance at the corpse-strewn beaches south of Garipadasi. This is why, according to Diodorus, the Athenians found fault with their leadership. But this evidence against an Athenian recovery effort is not compelling. Xenophon nowhere says that the Athenians left their dead unburied: for him, more plausibly, the chief concern of the Athenians back home was instead the failure of their commanders to rescue the survivors after the battle.[24]

Diodorus's insistence that all the dead of Arginusae were left unburied should not be taken seriously. That Xenophon and Diodorus fail to mention a recovery effort, meanwhile, does not imply that there wasn't one. As we've seen, their accounts of the Athenians' actions after the storm are severely truncated: there's a lot they haven't told us. Although there is no positive evidence for it, I think it likely that the Athenians did sail out after the storm to pick up their dead and rescue any sailors who were still alive. True, the delay caused by the storm meant they were less likely to find survivors, and many of the dead would no longer be floating. But there would still be corpses caught in the wreckage, and some may have washed ashore during the night. Collecting the bodies of men killed at sea the day after a battle may not have been ideal, but it wasn't unheard of: Thucydides tells us that the Corcyraeans collected bodies that had been scattered overnight in a wind storm the day after the Battle of Sybota in 433. And after a battle off Artemisium in 480, the bodies of men killed in the fight drifted around during the night, carried by a storm across the water, where they fouled the oars of the Persian ships at anchor. Since there was no urgent tactical reason for the Athenians to abandon the project of recovering their dead, it's hard to believe that they would have. My guess is that the forty-seven ships that had been tasked with the search and rescue before the storm undertook the project as soon as they could once the storm had passed. Meanwhile, the rest of the fleet sailed west toward Lesbos and met up somewhere along the way with Conon's thirty-eight ships.[25]

The Athenians may have collected their dead after the storm, but they probably didn't find very many survivors so late in the game. We hear of a guy who survived by clinging to a tub of barley, but for all we know he made it to shore on his own before the storm hit. Xenophon also says that one of the generals had to be rescued from a disabled ship, but we don't know at what point he was saved. It's possible that he and others were rescued after the battle but before the storm, when the ships were on their way back to Arginusae: the Athenians returned to the islands prior to organizing a rescue effort, but that doesn't mean they can't have picked up some survivors en route if they happened to pass any disabled ships. Some of the men in the water, then, ultimately made it to shore alive, but it was probably a very small percentage of the crewmen who had manned those twenty-five disabled ships. The number of fatalities on the Athenian side at Arginusae would therefore have approached five thousand men, some of them dead from wounds received in the battle itself, and some left to drown in the storm while the forty-seven ships tasked with rescuing them waited out the weather. The Athenians back home would have found it difficult to accept that many of those who died at Arginusae could have been saved if things had gone differently.[26]

-IV-

The Athenians and Their Generals: Democracy and Accountability

Wary of being bitten by their own magistrates, the *demos* at Athens ruled and kept its leaders on a tight leash—most of all, the generals, the only aristocratic or timocratic presence tolerated by the democratic regime.

Dustin Gish, "Defending *Dēmokratia*"

LATE IN THE SUMMER of 406, a month or more after the battle of Arginusae, the eight generals who had led the Athenian fleet to victory were removed from their commands and ordered to return to Athens. There, as we'll see, they would face questions concerning their conduct in office, a process that might result in disciplinary action of some kind or, if things went well, in their reinstatement to command. Six of the generals duly returned to answer to the Athenian people: Pericles, Diomedon, Lysias, Aristocrates, Thrasyllus, and Erasinides. But two generals, Protomachus and Aristogenes, refused the summons and, so far as we know, never went home again. Clearly, they weren't optimistic about their chances of successfully defending themselves before an angry electorate: Diodorus says outright that they fled because "they feared the wrath of the people." In chapter 5 we will discuss what happened after the battle that led to the generals' depositions and what proceedings were initiated against them after their return to Athens. And we will find out whether Protomachus and Aristogenes or their less panicky colleagues had more accurately gauged the temperament of the Athenian people. But to better appreciate the complicated series of events that would soon play out in

Athens, we should first discuss the peculiar brand of democracy the Athenians enjoyed and the means by which they monitored and disciplined the men elected to their state's most important office.[1]

Government by Amateurs

Athens' democracy was about a century old when the Battle of Arginusae was fought. The Athenians had ousted their tyrant Hippias in 510. A few years later, an aristocrat named Cleisthenes instituted a series of reforms that increased the authority of the demos—the mob of regular Joes who made up the bulk of the citizenry—at the expense of the aristocracy, thus leaving Athens a more democratic state. (*Democracy* derives from the Greek words *kratos*, "power," and *demos*, which can mean the citizen body generally, the Athenian assembly of citizens, or the common people, as opposed to the higher classes.) Cleisthenes reorganized the citizen body into ten new tribes from an earlier four. Unlike the previous tribes, which had been hereditary, these new tribes were based on geography. The state was divided into three broad geographical areas (the city, coastal, and inland regions), and each of these was in turn split into ten segments (*trittyes*). Three of these segments, one from each area, were combined to form a tribe. In this way, old allegiances were broken up, and new ties were formed among citizens from diverse parts of Attica. The organs of state—the courts, the council, the military, public offices—were now structured around the new tribes. The army, for example, was organized into ten tribal regiments, each commanded by an officer from that tribe. Men who died in battle were listed by tribe in inscriptions commemorating the fallen (see fig. 8).[2]

Among other reforms, Cleisthenes introduced a new council, or boule, whose duties included preparing the agenda for the assembly of citizens (*ekklesia*)—the principal decision-making body of the state. (All adult male citizens of Athens who had not lost their citizenship rights for some reason—such as for being in debt to the state—could participate in the *ekklesia*.) The boule considered in advance the matters that would be put to the people, sometimes merely introducing an item as a topic for debate, and sometimes offering concrete proposals that might then be ratified, revised, or rejected by the assembly. The council was composed of five hundred men, fifty chosen by lot from each tribe. In each of the council year's ten months (*prytaneiai*), the fifty members of one of the tribal contingents served as an executive board within the boule. The board members were called *prytaneis* and their period in office a *prytany*.

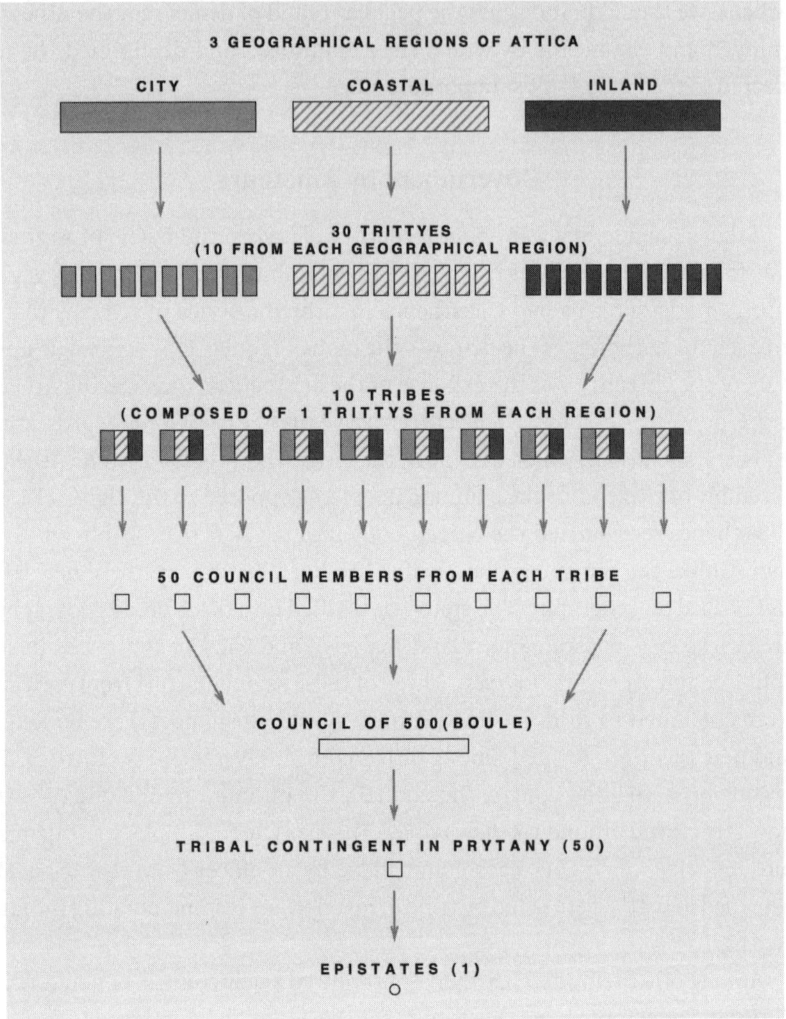

Figure 8. The composition of the tribes and the Council of 500 (boule) after Cleisthenes' reforms. © 2015 Debra Hamel

Every day, one member of the tribe that was in prytany was selected by lot to serve as chairman, or *epistates*, of the *prytaneis*. For twenty-four hours, from sunset to sunset, the *epistates* served as what amounted to Athens' head of state: he held the state seal and the keys to Athens' treasuries, and he had to remain on duty for the day in the *prytaneis*' headquarters, a round building called the *tholos* in the Athenian agora (the city's marketplace or public square).

A man could serve on the Athenian boule twice in his lifetime, though in nonconsecutive years, but he could serve as *epistates* of the *prytaneis* only once.[3]

The experience of the *epistates* illustrates a fundamental peculiarity of Athens' democracy. Here was a man who, at least on paper, was no more or less qualified than any other Athenian citizen to fulfill the responsibilities of his office. He was selected by lot from a body of fifty men who had likewise been selected by lot to serve on a board of five hundred. He could serve for only a limited time on the boule and for an even briefer period as chairman of that board. He thus could not develop any particular competence at the job or become entrenched in office. The *epistates* was, in short, an amateur, and the same was true of most of those who served as public officials in Athens. In addition to the five hundred men who served on the boule every year, there were some seven hundred other officials in Athens, most of whom were, like the councilors, selected by lot. Most of the offices they filled could be held only once, and most were collegiate, boards of five or ten or more men overseeing some small slice of public business. The *Athenaion Politeia*—a history of Athens' political system written in the fourth century B.C. by Aristotle or one of his students—lists among the officials of the author's day, for example, five commissioners of the roads, who oversaw the slaves who repaired the roadways, ten officials in charge of making the sacrifices that had been prescribed by oracles, eleven men charged with supervising the prisons and performing executions (the so-called Eleven), and ten city commissioners, whose jobs were manifold and weird. They were tasked with making sure that Athens' flute girls—musically adept, relatively inexpensive prostitutes—weren't being paid too much and that the dung collectors weren't depositing their loads too close to the city walls. They also had to remove the corpses of anyone who happened to die in the street.[4]

The extent to which the Athenians relied on amateurs to run their state may strike us moderns as madness, and the practice had its detractors in antiquity as well. Socrates reportedly disapproved of selecting officials by lot: you wouldn't hire just anyone to build your house or pilot your ship, his argument went; why then would you put the state in the hands of men who lacked experience?[5] Leaving the selection of magistrates to chance would certainly have been ill advised if the Athenians' goal was to find the most competent man for a job or if the position he was to fill required above average ability. But in most cases neither was true. As the examples cited above suggest, most of the jobs that needed doing didn't require any unusual competence: it didn't take a brain surgeon, after all, to check up on the dung collector. The average Athenian, in other words, was in most cases good enough. Having rid their state of tyrants in the late sixth century, moreover, and with bitter memories in particular of the latter years of Hippias's reign, the Athenians were deeply reluctant to allow too much power to be concentrated in the hands of any one individual. By selecting most of their officials by lot to collegiate offices with limited terms, the Athenians diminished the potential power of their magistrates.

The Athenians' reliance on amateurs only went so far, however. They weren't crazy enough—or sufficiently confident of the competency of average Athenians—to entrust important military positions (and a handful of other vital jobs) to men whose names had been drawn at random. The Athenian generalship (*strategia*), in particular, was an elective office throughout the classical period. A board of ten generals (*strategoi*) was elected every spring in a special meeting of the assembly—which met in the open air, on a hill called the Pnyx, about a half mile west of the Acropolis. Perhaps some six thousand men would have been in attendance on election day, crammed into a space about half the size of an American football field. The method of voting used in the assembly was low-tech even by ancient standards. The Athenians decided most matters of state, and they elected their generals, by show of hands (*cheirotonia*), and so far as we know, those hands were never counted: a rough estimate of raised appendages decided the matter. Like many other officials, the generals were originally elected one from each tribe, but this system was later abandoned: after (probably) the mid-fifth century, the generals were elected from the whole citizen body, so that a single tribe might furnish two or more generals in any given year.[6]

Athens' generals, then, were unusual in being elected to office rather than selected by lot. They also differed from most other public officials in another important respect. The Athenians recognized that limiting the number of skilled military commanders available to them by instituting term limits would have been unwise. Thus, while most magistracies could be held only once, and citizens could serve in the boule no more than twice, generals could be reelected to office repeatedly. At least half of the men who commanded at Arginusae, for example, had also served as generals in previous years.[7]

Pragmatism thus compelled the Athenians to exempt their generals from some of the constraints they imposed on other officials. As a result, the generals were in a unique position in Athenian society. The fact of their election implied that they enjoyed some degree of popularity in the state; they could potentially hold their positions indefinitely; and the nature of their job meant that they were invested with an unusual degree of authority over important matters. Generals were, moreover, dispatched from Athens with armies at their backs—just the sort of thing that could lead to a military coup under the right circumstances. The generalship thus represented a potential threat to Athens' democracy.

Civilian Oversight of the Military

When generals sailed off from Athens en route to some theater of war or other, they did so with the instructions of the assembly ringing in their ears. Sometimes the people's directives were quite specific. In 433, for example, shortly before the Peloponnesian War began, three generals were dispatched to Corcyra to help the island in its war against Corinth. The situation at the time was tense. The Corcyraeans had sent ambassadors to ask the Athenians for help and an alliance. But Corinth was a member of Sparta's Peloponnesian League, and the Thirty Years' Peace, which had ended the First Peloponnesian War back in 446/5, was still in effect. If the Athenians helped the Corcyraeans by attacking Corinthian forces outright, they would be in breach of the treaty. They therefore agreed only to a defensive alliance with Corcyra, and they gave their generals precise instructions about the conditions under which they could engage the Corinthians: "The Athenians ordered them not to attack the Corinthians unless they sailed against Corcyra or one of its territories and were about to make a landing. If that happened they could use force to prevent it." The generals who were sent to Sicily in 415 were likewise dispatched with specific directives, but at the same time they were explicitly given the latitude to make decisions themselves about the conduct of the campaign. They were sent, Thucydides writes, "as allies to the Egestaeans against the Selinuntines, and, if they had the advantage in the war, they were to resettle the Leontinians, and with respect to other matters in Sicily to do whatever they thought best for Athens."[8]

In addition to issuing instructions to generals prior to their departure from Athens, the Athenians also remained in contact with their commanders while they were away, receiving communications from the field and sometimes issuing additional instructions midcampaign. The large number of references in our sources to communication of both types suggests that the Athenians were typically aware of and involved in what their generals were up to out in the field.[9]

During the fourth century the Athenians had mechanisms in place for regularly scrutinizing their officials while they were in office. A board of ten auditors was selected by lot from the boule to inspect the officials' financial accounts every prytany. And there was a mandatory vote in the assembly every month on the magistrates' performance in office. Any citizen who wished could propose that a vote of no confidence be held against one of the state's officials. If the vote went against the magistrate, he would be deposed from office (by *apocheirotonia*) and tried. We don't know what procedures were in place for midterm scrutiny in the fifth century, but it's clear, whatever the specifics, that the Athenians had some mechanism for deposing generals at least as early as 430/29, when the elder Pericles was removed from office.[10]

Starting in about 460, magistrates also underwent a final audit once their terms had been completed. Like the monthly checks described above, this last procedure, the *euthyna*, was an examination into the officials' overall conduct in office as well as their handling of any public moneys entrusted to them. The procedure offered a further opportunity for anyone who wished to charge the official with misbehavior related to his magistracy. Unless they were deemed unjustified, complaints raised against officials at their *euthynae* would lead to legal action.[11]

The Athenians also exercised another, more subtle check on the conduct of their commanders. While they were away from Athens, generals were surrounded at all times by other Athenian citizens—their colleagues in the generalship, subordinate military officers, and many of the soldiers and oarsmen they commanded. These officers and citizen soldiers were thus first-hand witnesses to a general's conduct on campaign, and they could, as constituent members of the demos, testify against or prosecute him once they'd returned to Athens. We hear of a number of cases in which precisely this happened. In 393/2, for example, the Athenian general Conon—the same man who was blockaded in Mytilene in 406—prosecuted his fellow general Adeimantus in connection with their shared command at Aegospotami in 405/4. In 360/59 a trierarch, Apollodorus, likewise brought accusations against three generals he had served under in 362/1 and 361/0. Soldiers who were dissatisfied with their general's performance could also threaten his career less directly, injuring his reputation by sharing their campaign experiences with family and friends. A general who had alienated a substantial number of his men was unlikely to be reelected to the generalship. The constant presence on campaign of a slice of the Athenian electorate, all of them potential witnesses for the prosecution, would have served, I suggest, as an additional check on a generals' behavior, a further incentive for him to obey his orders and otherwise act in accordance with the expectations of the Athenian demos.[12]

Known Trials and Sentences

The Athenians, as we've seen, had procedures in place for regularly scrutinizing their officials and prosecuting anyone against whom legitimate accusations were brought. But these mechanisms would not have served to deter generals from acting against the will of the people unless they were seen to have bite—unless, that is, complaints of malfeasance regularly resulted in prosecution and the imposition of severe penalties. Unfortunately, we don't have enough evidence to come to any conclusions about the frequency or severity of disciplinary action taken against generals in the first two-thirds of the fifth century. Our evidence for the Peloponnesian War years is somewhat fuller. We know of nine cases in which generals were prosecuted in connection with their generalships between 431 and the summer of 406—that is, from the beginning of the Peloponnesian War to shortly before the Battle of Arginusae:

— 430/29: Pericles was deposed, found guilty, and fined.
— 429/8: Phormio—whom we last saw in chapter 2, commanding a squadron of twenty ships in the Corinthian Gulf—was found guilty and fined.
— 428/7: Paches—who came within a hair's breadth of having to execute the entire male population of Mytilene—reportedly killed himself at his *euthyna*. The story is probably apocryphal, but it suggests that Paches was tried in connection with his generalship and perhaps found guilty.
— 425/4: Eurymedon was found guilty and fined.
— 425/4: Pythodorus and Sophocles, who had been serving with Eurymedon in Sicily, went into exile. This may have been the penalty imposed on them, or they may have fled before trial, in which case they would likely have been sentenced to death in absentia. (This is not the Sophocles who wrote *Oedipus Rex*, but the more famous Sophocles did serve as general in Athens in 441/0.)
— 424/3: Thucydides, the author of the *History of the Peloponnesian War*, was held responsible for the Athenians' loss of Amphipolis. It's likely that he never returned for trial and was consequently sentenced to death in absentia.
— 411: Aristarchus was tried sometime between 411 and 406 for his betrayal of Oenoe in 411. He was found guilty and executed. (One could argue, however, that Aristarchus was not acting in his capacity as a

general on this occasion, but rather as an agent of the oligarchic regime that had just been deposed.)

— 409/8: Anytus was tried and acquitted.

These, at least, are the trials for which we have reasonably good evidence. It is very likely, however, that more generals were prosecuted between 431 and 406 than the nine our sources happen to reference in any detail.[13]

The trials listed above are distributed fairly evenly across the twenty-five-year period between 431 and 406—with a noticeable gap during those years in which Athens and Sparta were ostensibly at peace (421–413). (The Athenians fought at Mantinea in 418, and they were active in Sicily between 415 and 413, but in both cases the generals who were in command—Laches and Nicostratus at Mantinea, Nicias, Lamachus, Demosthenes, and Eurymedon in Sicily—were all killed in battle or executed by the enemy after capture.) The prosecution of generals thus seems to have been a regular feature of the war years—regular enough, at any rate, for the possibility of prosecution to have loomed as a very real threat to Athens' commanders. Nor were the punishments meted out in these cases insignificant. Of the nine generals listed above only one, admittedly, was executed, and his was arguably a special case. But three of the remaining generals appear to have fled into exile, with a standing death sentence hanging over their heads should they return to Athens. This was not a trivial penalty: Thucydides, we know, remained in exile for twenty years (a misfortune which, however, afforded him the opportunity to research and write his magnum opus). As for the generals who were fined, we don't know the amount of the penalty imposed on Eurymedon, but Pericles, by all accounts, was forced to cough up a fortune: the smallest figure our sources report for his fine is fifteen talents, a sum it would take an oarsman of the day several lifetimes to earn. Phormio was fined a much smaller amount (a hundred *minae*, or 1.67 talents), but it was more than he could pay: he became a debtor to the state and consequently lost his citizenship rights. In short, our evidence suggests that, at least during the Peloponnesian War years, generals were prosecuted frequently, and most of those who were brought to trial were in turn convicted. Once convicted, they were punished severely.[14]

Fear of Punishment

Those three generals who were dispatched to Corcyra in 433 with precise instructions about when they could engage the enemy ultimately failed to do as they were told. They had been ordered not to attack the Corinthians unless they attempted a landing on Corcyraean territory. In theory, staying out of the fight was easily done, but the reality was different. The Corcyraeans had 110 ships in the water against a Corinthian fleet of 150. Once the signals were raised on either side, chaos reigned. It was an old-fashioned battle in which the sophisticated tactics that Athens' fleet used to such advantage were not tried. Instead, the fighting was hand-to-hand—marines on blood-drenched decks thrusting with spears and swords. All the while the ten Athenian ships that were on hand tried to help their allies without coming to blows with the Corinthians: "The Athenian ships came up to the Corcyraeans wherever they were hard pressed," Thucydides tells us, "and they alarmed the enemy, but the generals did not join the battle, as they were afraid of the instructions of the Athenians." Finally, however, the generals could no longer stay their hands. The Athenians wound up joining the fight rather than sitting idly by while their allies were destroyed:

> The Athenians, seeing the Corcyraeans hard pressed, gave their help more openly. At first they refrained from attacking anyone, but when it was clearly a rout and the Corinthians were winning, then everyone joined in and there was no further distinction, but it got to the point that the Corinthians and Athenians attacked one another.

Despite this outcome, Thucydides' description of the generals' hesitant participation in the fighting makes it clear that they did not take the instructions of the Athenian people lightly. Indeed, Thucydides—who knew something himself about the potential ramifications of failing the Athenian demos—explicitly says that the generals' fear of the Athenians made them loath to join the fight.[15]

Other passages likewise suggest that Athens' generals nurtured a healthy fear of disappointing the Athenians back home. In the summer of 426, Demosthenes led an invasion into Aetolia in central Greece. The campaign turned into a debacle in which the Athenians met with "every form of death." Specifically, some 120 Athenian hoplites were killed—the finest men from Athens to die in the war, Thucydides tells us. Demosthenes' fellow general Procles was also killed in Aetolia, along with many of Athens' allies. When the fighting was done, the Athenians collected their dead under truce and retired to Naupactus, on the Corinthian Gulf, and from there returned to Athens. Demosthenes, however, stayed behind. Thucydides says he was afraid of the Athenians because of what had happened. As far as we know, Demosthenes was not deposed from his command. Thucydides' account suggests that his failure to return to Athens was precautionary rather than a response to his being recalled.

Whatever the particulars, Demosthenes put his period of self-imposed exile to good use. Later that summer, when he was no longer general, he saved Naupactus from being captured by the Spartans. And in the winter he led the Acarnanians of central Greece—they had invited him to serve as their commander—to a pair of victories against the Spartans and their allies. The Acarnanians gave Demosthenes a hefty share of the spoils from these battles: three hundred suits of armor. He returned with them to Athens, where, in a politic gesture, he dedicated them in various temples. "Because of this exploit," Thucydides writes, "he was less afraid of returning to Athens after the disaster in Aetolia." As it turned out, Demosthenes was right to suspect that his successes in central Greece—and the three hundred panoplies he brought home with him—would appease the Athenians. As far as we know, he was not punished for his part in the Aetolian disaster. Indeed, he was elected to the generalship again in 425: in the spring of that year, while he was general elect, Demosthenes would bring about the fortification of Pylos.[16]

A dozen years later, in the final months of the Athenians' Sicilian Expedition, Demosthenes was dispatched to the island with a relief force of seventy-three ships. He was determined to take decisive action against the Syracusans at once, while the Athenians on the scene were buoyed by his arrival and the enemy correspondingly dispirited. With a view to capturing Syracuse, he organized a daring nighttime attack on Epipolae, the heights overlooking the city, but the assault ended badly. In the darkness the Athenians couldn't tell friend from foe, and they wound up killing one another accidentally. They were also less familiar with the terrain than the enemy: they got lost and wandered around until they were dispatched by Syracusan cavalry, or they fell off the cliffs of Epipolae to their deaths. Afterwards, Demosthenes wanted the Athenians to cut their losses and withdraw from Sicily at once, but Nicias, his fellow general, disagreed. He had his reasons. For one thing, he was in communication with sympathizers inside the city who were looking to betray Syracuse to the Athenians. But Nicias was also concerned about how the people back home would respond if he and Demosthenes pulled out of Sicily on their own initiative. He was certain the Athenians would disapprove, and that some clever speaker would persuade them to condemn the generals. What's more, Nicias said, the men whom he and Demosthenes commanded, who were witness to what was going on in Sicily and knew full well the dire position they were in, would turn on them once they reached Athens:

> Many of the soldiers who are here—indeed, the majority of them—who now cry out that they are in terrible straits, will say the opposite when they get to Athens, that their generals betrayed them and withdrew because they were bribed. I myself, knowing the Athenian character, do not want to be put to death unjustly by the Athenians on some disgraceful charge, but I would prefer, if need be, risking that same fate at the hands of the enemy, to suffer it on my own terms.

Thus the Athenians stayed on, and the Sicilian Expedition soon ended in the annihilation of Athens' entire expeditionary force. Nicias's fear of the demos—justified, no doubt, but hardly commendable—was a primary factor in the Athenians' loss of more than a hundred ships and many thousands of men. The Athenians' penchant for punishing magistrates who had disappointed them may have served as an effective check on the power of individuals, ensuring that the demos remained the ultimate authority in the state. But as the Sicilian Expedition demonstrates, their disciplinary verve could backfire on them—in this case prompting their military commanders to make what appeared to be safe decisions rather than smart ones.[17]

It remains to consider the one anomaly in that list of trials in our last section: unlike the other generals who were prosecuted between 431 and 406, Anytus, who was charged with treason in the winter of 409/8, was acquitted. Anytus had been dispatched from Athens with a fleet of thirty ships to bring help to the garrison at Pylos, which was defending the fort against a Spartan siege. But Anytus never made it beyond Cape Malea, the tip of the easternmost finger of the Peloponnese. According to Diodorus, he was unable to round the promontory because of storms. Presumably this was the defense Anytus made at his trial, and, on the face of it, at least, the claim is credible. Strong winds are common in the area, especially during the winter: modern measurements show that winds of twenty-two knots or more (Beaufort force 6) occur near the Cape on an average of twelve days each in December and January—hard sailing for an ancient trireme. Literary evidence suggests that the hazards of rounding the Cape were notorious in antiquity. Homer and Herodotus tell of a number of ancient heroes—Menelaus, Agamemnon, Odysseus, and Jason—who were allegedly blown off course when sailing near Malea. And the geographer Strabo preserves a proverb that hints at the uneasiness with which sailors approached the Cape: "Round Malea and forget about home." (Lionel Casson mentions an interesting modern-day parallel: until recently, he writes, modern Greek sailors would sing, "Cape Malea, Cape Malea; help me Christ and all the Saints!") Earlier in the fifth century, meanwhile, the Corcyraeans had cited their inability to round the Cape as the reason for their failure to help the Greeks at Salamis. That the difficulty of navigating around Malea was well known may explain why Anytus was acquitted at his trial: the jurors who heard his case, after all, were Athenians. If they were not oarsmen or marines or rowing masters or ships' captains themselves, they still, by virtue of their residence in Attica, lived lives connected with the sea. They voted for naval expenditures in the assembly and sat next to sailors in the Theater of Dionysus. They knew their Homer, too, and they doubtless knew—whether firsthand or secondhand or from the Homeric stories they were suckled on—of the troubles that plagued sailors around Malea: Anytus's defense, I should think, would not have been lightly dismissed.[18]

Anytus was tried only a few years before Arginusae. His acquittal, and the fact that he had successfully blamed bad weather for his failure to save Pylos, may have seemed like a hopeful precedent to the six generals who returned to Athens in 406. Surely the Athenian people could be made to understand that they too had been helpless in the face of a tempest. On the other hand, there was a rumor circulating about Anytus's acquittal, disquieting whispers that told a less hopeful story. Anytus, some said, had escaped conviction only because he'd bribed the jury. The story may not have been true. The sheer size of Athenian juries—501 men in Anytus's case—would have made bribery almost impossibly difficult: Anytus was allegedly the first man to have managed it. But the accusation is telling whether or not it is true. Generals who were prosecuted in the late fifth century were not expected to be acquitted. Had the Arginusae generals pondered Anytus's case for too long, then, they might have wondered if their decision to return to Athens when summoned was wise.[19]

-V-

The Aftermath in Athens: Tribunals and Tribulations

We tend nowadays to associate democracy with tolerance, forgetting that a majority is quite capable of making and enforcing much more repressive laws than an easy-going autocrat. We also tend to imagine that democracies are by nature lenient in punishment and reluctant to take the lives of their own citizens. If we have made this assumption, the conduct of the classical Athenian democracy will sometimes surprise us.

Kenneth Dover, *Greek Popular Morality in the Time of Plato and Aristotle*

AT THE END OF CHAPTER 3 we left the Athenian fleet divided and attending to separate tasks in the Aegean. Forty-seven ships under the command of the trierarchs Theramenes and Thrasybulus undertook a belated rescue and recovery mission—or so I've argued—while the rest of the fleet sailed to Mytilene and then against Chios. We know that the eight generals who had commanded at Arginusae were deposed and recalled to Athens, but that didn't happen immediately. The battle was fought in late July or early August, and the generals were summoned back to Athens probably in early to mid-September. Neither of our principal sources for these events provides a fully satisfactory account of what happened leading up to the generals' recall. Xenophon's narrative jumps abruptly from the immediate aftermath of the battle to the Athenians' summons, which obscures the fact that a month or more had passed in the interim and suggests that the deposition of the generals came out of nowhere. Xenophon provides information later in his narrative that fills in this gap to an extent, but as we'll see, his account still needs to be supplemented with information from Diodorus in order for it to make sense. Diodorus, meanwhile, provides an inherently coherent narrative—in his account the deposition of the generals is intelligible—but he doesn't tell us everything we'd like to know. I attempt below to reconstruct the events that culminated in the deposition of the generals, supplementing the information provided by our sources with educated guesswork when necessary. (See Appendix A for a timeline summarizing my conclusions about the sequence of events.) Once we've discussed why the generals were deposed, we'll look in detail at what happened after they returned to Athens—a complicated series of events that snowballed into something grimmer and more lastingly significant than any of the participants in the process likely anticipated or wanted.[1]

Ashes and Dispatches

One of the first things the generals who commanded at Arginusae would have wanted to do after the battle was to let the Athenians back home know what had happened. Xenophon tells us they sent a letter to the demos and boule in which they "blamed nothing other than the storm." The generals' letter, then, must have contained some reference to the fleet's failure to retrieve the corpses and rescue the shipwrecked survivors of the battle in a timely fashion. I would assume that the letter also included an account of the bare facts of the engagement, with an estimate of the number of Spartan ships destroyed and an accurate count of the number of Athenian triremes lost. The vessels that had not returned to Arginusae after the battle may in fact have been identified by name in the letter. The number of casualties sustained and the names of the dead may not yet have been known at the time the letter was sent, but a list of the ships lost and the generals' description of the storm's ferocity would have given the demos a sense of the probable death toll. The letter would also have alerted the families of those whose ships were lost to the likelihood of their loved ones' deaths. What was *not* in the generals' letter was any reference to Theramenes and Thrasybulus having been tasked with picking up the dead and shipwrecked. At the urging of two of their number—Diomedon and Pericles—the generals left that detail out of their report. The fact of the trierarchs' assignment would inevitably become known in Athens, of course, but the generals were apparently making a conscious effort not to suggest in their letter that Theramenes and Thrasybulus were in any way culpable for the losses sustained after the battle: the storm, and only the storm, was to blame.[2]

My guess is that this letter was sent to Athens while the trierarchs and the men they commanded were still hauling in bodies. The job would have taken some time. The forty-seven ships assigned to the task probably crisscrossed the waters around Arginusae for several days at least—towing disabled vessels back to the island (and extracting bodies from them when necessary), combing the seas around Arginusae for floaters, visiting the beaches south of the islands and collecting any corpses that had washed ashore. If only half the Athenian dead were ultimately recovered, that still amounts to some 2500 corpses, in various stages of decay, that needed to be manhandled aboard the rescue ships and brought to shore—a backbreaking and unimaginably dreadful task for the unfortunates who'd been given the job. The dead were presumably gathered in piles on Arginusae, identified if possible, and burned en masse: the great number of corpses that needed to be dealt with surely precluded individual cremations. The remains would then have been collected and stored for transport. Even reduced to ash and bone, the bodies of 2500 men would have weighed a fair amount—some 13,000 pounds, by my estimation (the equivalent of about eighty-eight live oarsmen), and that's not counting the weight of whatever vessels the remains were stored in. The ashes would have taken up quite a bit of room as well—370,000 cubic inches, or about eight cubic yards, or just over 1600 gallons. (Eight cubic yards, by the way, is a standard dumpster size. If you search for images of eight-yard dumpsters online, you'll get a good sense of the volume we're talking about.) Given their weight and volume, the remains were probably divided for transport among several triremes. Once the job of finding and burning the dead was finished, the rescue ships—some of them, at least (see below)—would have returned to the Athenians' base at Samos, towing behind them any wrecks they had found that were deemed salvageable, whether Athenian or Peloponnesian. At Samos they would reunite with the rest of the fleet, which likewise headed back to base after an unsuccessful attack on Chios.[3]

Diodorus tells us that Thrasybulus and Theramenes returned to Athens before the rest of the fleet. He doesn't tell us why they did so, however, and most modern accounts of the Arginusae affair offer no explanation for their early homecoming. Donald Kagan is unusual in considering the question: "Theramenes and Thrasybulus had hurried home after their return to Samos," he writes. "No doubt they realized that theirs was the most vulnerable position and were eager to defend themselves if necessary." But there was as yet no intimation that the trierarchs might be blamed for the high casualties incurred at Arginusae. And even if they *were* eager to defend themselves, their anxiety cannot adequately explain their return: it was the middle of campaign season, and the trierarchs were on active duty in the Aegean. They must have been on some official business—or have been officially excused from service for some reason—when they sailed to Athens. I would suggest that their return was connected with the task they'd been assigned, that they sailed to Athens, probably accompanied by a small fleet for their protection, to bring the remains of the dead home. They may have left for Athens straight from Arginusae, in fact, after sending some of the rescue ships south, wrecks in tow, to rendezvous with the rest of the fleet at Samos. It's impossible to know whether it was standard procedure for the Athenians to ship the remains of their dead home immediately after a battle. Perhaps, if there were few fatalities, the ashes were instead stored for a time until they could be put aboard the next dispatch boat bound for Athens—no separate trip necessary. But the death toll at Arginusae was so high, and the remains of the dead so voluminous, that sending the ashes home at once made sense: there was no point in lugging them to Samos for temporary storage. As I see it, then, the trierarchs' return to Athens can be fully explained as the final task in their rescue and recovery mission. It need not have resulted from any anxiety on their part about their job performance: they, after all, had done nothing wrong.[4]

At some point—probably before the trierarchs made it back to Athens—the Athenians received the generals' letter detailing what had happened in the battle. It's hard to fully appreciate how relieved they must have been at the news. The scratch fleet they had thrown together in a month, manning their ships with anyone, slave or free, who was fit for service, had managed against all odds to destroy some seventy Peloponnesian ships and to free Conon from the blockade at Mytilene. In doing so, the Athenians had probably saved their city from total defeat in the war, the likely result of a Spartan win at Arginusae. But victory had come at a high price. The Athenians' joy at their reprieve would have been mingled with grief and, even at this early stage, perhaps tinged with anger over the losses sustained: as we saw in chapter 4, the Athenians tended to look for scapegoats when military engagements ended less than satisfactorily. The trierarchs' arrival in Athens soon afterwards with casualty lists and triremes laden with the ashes of dead Athenians would have further aroused any simmering dissatisfaction over the way things had been handled at Arginusae. There were rumblings of discontent, apparently—some sign, at any rate, that the demos was less than happy with the leadership of its generals. Eventually, word of this worsening mood in Athens made its way overseas to the fleet at Samos—just talk, nothing official yet, probably carried via dispatch boat or merchant ship by men on unrelated business.[5]

When the generals heard that the mood in Athens had turned against them, they assumed, not unreasonably given the sequence of events, that Theramenes and Thrasybulus were responsible: the trierarchs, the generals supposed, were slandering them behind their backs. The generals consequently took up their styluses and dashed off another letter or letters—Diodorus uses the plural—to the demos. Having omitted any reference to the trierarchs' assignment in their first letter, the generals now "made it very clear" that they had ordered Theramenes and Thrasybulus to "pick up the dead."[6] (Xenophon does not mention these letters, but their existence is consistent with his account. Indeed, as we'll see below, his narrative makes more sense if we assume the letters were sent.) By this time the Athenians must already have known about the trierarchs' rescue and recovery mission: after all, Theramenes and Thrasybulus were back in Athens with six and a half tons of human remains—or so I've argued—as well as hundreds of sailors, who are unlikely to have kept quiet about the tasks they'd been assigned after the battle. So the generals' news was no news, really—unless they had more dirt to dish than Diodorus tells us. What *was* new was that the generals were now pointing fingers. The underlying message of their correspondence seems to have been that if the *kopros* was going to hit the fan over this issue, the Athenians should take a good look at the trierarchs and not blame the generals for what had happened.

Sometime later, the generals' letters were read out in the assembly. When they heard them, the people were angry at Theramenes and Thrasybulus, but the trierarchs defended themselves: we don't know what they said—perhaps, as has been suggested, they blamed the generals for not giving the orders to mount a rescue operation sooner. But whatever their defense, they successfully deflected the blame from themselves. The Athenians, angry anew at their generals, resolved to depose them and recall them to Athens.[7]

The Trial of the Generals

As we've seen, two of the generals who had commanded at Arginusae, Protomachus and Aristogenes, chose to go into exile rather than return to Athens when summoned; we don't know what ultimately became of them. The other six generals sailed home from Samos, evidently more sanguine than their colleagues about their chances back in Athens. Xenophon provides a detailed account of what happened after their return. The proceedings against them developed by stages, in different venues, and over the course of many days—a complicated and lengthy business, interrupted by debates over procedure and, on one occasion, by nightfall. We'll discuss each step in detail below. (The events are also summarized in Appendix B.)[8]

Erasinides

The first legal action taken after the generals returned to Athens was initiated by a man named Archedemus, a popular political figure of the day who held some kind of financial office that year: he was in charge of the "two-obol fund," Xenophon tells us, though it's not clear precisely what that was. According to Xenophon, Archedemus imposed a fine on one of the generals, Erasinides—presumably whatever office Archedemus held gave him the authority to do so—and he accused Erasinides of embezzlement in a court of law: "He said that Erasinides had money from the Hellespont that belonged to the demos." Xenophon doesn't make this clear, but it makes sense to assume, as Martin Ostwald suggests, that the court became involved in Erasinides' case only after he contested his fine. Archedemus also accused Erasinides in court "concerning his generalship." We know nothing further about this latter charge: it may or may not have had anything to do with what happened at Arginusae. In the end, the court voted to imprison Erasinides, but this would not have been his punishment, exactly. The Athenians did not ordinarily impose imprisonment as a penalty during this period. Instead, they fined or exiled or executed the guilty, or they might confiscate their property or take away their citizenship rights. Prisons could be used, however, to hold defendants prior to trial to prevent their flight or, similarly, to prevent anyone who had been condemned to death from taking off before he could be executed. Socrates, famously, was imprisoned in Athens for about a month pending his execution by hemlock poisoning in 399. Debtors to the state were also sometimes imprisoned until they could pay what they owed. In the case of Erasinides, the court probably upheld the fine imposed by Archedemus and imprisoned Erasinides as a debtor because he was unable to pay it.[9]

A number of scholars have suggested that Erasinides was the first of the generals to be attacked because he was viewed as "uniquely guilty or, at least, more guilty than the others," as Donald Kagan puts it. Erasinides, you may remember, was the general who reportedly argued after the battle that the Athenians should sail to Mytilene at once, which would have meant abandoning those who had been shipwrecked to their fate. Erasinides' unique guiltiness may indeed have prompted Archedemus's attack, but it's more than our sources tell us. After all, we can't even be sure that Erasinides' trial was connected in any way with Arginusae. But only a few months later, early in 405, Archedemus was lampooned in Aristophanes' *Frogs* as being "tops at villainy." Aristophanes' hostility suggests that by the time the play was produced, Archedemus's attack on Erasinides was perceived, at least, as being connected with the regrettable events that occurred afterwards.[10]

The First Meeting of the Boule

Sometime after Erasinides' imprisonment, the generals reported to the boule, describing the battle at Arginusae and the magnitude of the storm that had come up afterwards. On the motion of one of the councilors, Timocrates, the boule decided to hand the generals over to the assembly, which would then determine what subsequent procedures, if any, would be used against them. The boule also decided to imprison the generals pending any further decision in their case.[11]

The First Assembly Meeting

An assembly meeting followed at which, per the instructions of the boule, the matter of the Arginusae generals came up for discussion. During the meeting, a number of people—and the trierarch Theramenes especially—spoke out against the generals and said they should be made "to render an account because they had not picked up the shipwrecked." The language Xenophon uses for "render an account" (*logon huposchein*) suggests that Theramenes was proposing specifically that the generals be required to undergo the *euthyna*, the investigative procedure mentioned in our last chapter to which all outgoing officials in Athens were regularly subjected. We'll come back to the potential significance of Theramenes' call for an *euthyna* later in this chapter. Xenophon also tells us that Theramenes showed the assembled Athenians the first letter the generals had sent home, in which they had not mentioned the trierarchs but had "blamed nothing other than the storm." As others have pointed out, it doesn't make sense for Theramenes to mention this letter in the context of an attack on the generals: Theramenes seems rather to be defending himself. Xenophon doesn't give us any reason to think that Theramenes should be on the defensive, but as we've seen, Diodorus does: that second batch of letters the generals sent in which they "made it very clear" that the trierarchs had been tasked with rescue and recovery after Arginusae. Xenophon's account thus makes better sense if we assume that those letters were indeed sent.[12]

After Theramenes and the others had had their say, each of the generals addressed the assembly. They explained now in person what they had written in their letters, that they had assigned the task of recovering the shipwrecked to Theramenes and Thrasybulus, among others. If someone had to be blamed for what had happened after Arginusae, they said, one would have to fault the men who'd been given the job. But the generals also explicitly absolved those men of any wrongdoing. Although the trierarchs had blamed them, they explained, they weren't going to lie and say that the trierarchs were culpable: the ferocity of the storm was what had prevented the rescue.[13] The position the generals now took was thus an amalgam of what they'd said in their earlier communications to the demos, blaming the storm (as in the first letter) while making it clear that the rescue mission had been the trierarchs' responsibility and not theirs (the letters mentioned by Diodorus). The generals' position on the trierarch's culpability seems to have been both more nuanced and less hostile than the one they had adopted in their last letters home.

The generals brought forward as witnesses a number of men who'd served at Arginusae, "helmsmen and many other of their fellow sailors." The generals' testimony, and that of their witnesses, reportedly had the desired effect. Xenophon writes that "they were persuading the demos," and that many of the citizens wanted to stand surety for the generals. This means that they offered to stand as guarantors of the generals' appearance at trial—rather like posting bail for someone in the modern world—which would mean that the generals would be freed from prison in the interim. But however persuasive the generals and their witnesses may have been, real life intervened to put a brake on their momentum. We mentioned above that voting in the assembly was usually by show of hands. The problem with this method of decision-making was that it couldn't be done in the dark: there was no stadium lighting in antiquity. The assembly had gone long and there wasn't enough light for a count, so the Athenians resolved to postpone the Arginusae business to another meeting and to pass the ball back to the boule: they ordered the councilors to deliberate and come up with a proposal regarding how the generals should be tried.[14]

One question about the trial of the generals that we'll keep coming back to is whether the proceedings were conducted throughout in accordance with the law. Some scholars have seen evidence of illegality in this first meeting of the assembly. The question hinges on our understanding of a single phrase in Xenophon's account. Xenophon says that at the meeting the generals each spoke briefly in their defense, and he explains in a parenthetical comment why their remarks were brief: "for a speech was not permitted them in accordance with the law." Xenophon's Greek is ambiguous, as is my translation of it. Does it mean that by law the generals should have been given the opportunity to make a full speech, but they were not? Or were they not allowed by law to make a full speech in their defense at a regular assembly meeting? Martin Ostwald argues that the second interpretation is preferable, since Xenophon's account does not otherwise suggest that the generals were being treated unfairly on this occasion. Indeed, Xenophon suggests that the generals, far from being victimized through an illegal curtailment of their rights, were in fact winning the day with their brief arguments and the corroborating testimony of the witnesses they were allowed to call. I agree with Ostwald in preferring the second interpretation of Xenophon's ambiguous sentence and in concluding that, as yet, at least, nothing illegal had taken place.[15]

The Apaturia

There was a delay of at least several days before the boule could meet to consider the Arginusae matter for the second time. This is because the festival of the Apaturia was celebrated shortly after the first assembly meeting (roughly in mid-October), and the boule was not usually called during festival days. The Apaturia was in essence a celebration of family. All male citizens of Athens belonged to a phratry, a group of people who were or were believed to be distantly related to one another. There may have been a hundred or more such groups in Athens. During the Apaturia these kinship groups would get together for three days of celebrations. The festivities culminated in a kind of induction ceremony, when fathers would register their young sons in the phratry.[16]

According to Xenophon, Theramenes used the opportunity of the Apaturia to stir up popular feeling against the generals: "At the festival Theramenes and his supporters arranged with a large number of men, wearing black cloaks and with their hair shaved close, that they would go to the assembly as if they were relatives of the dead." Theramenes, in other words, was allegedly trying to poison the atmosphere of the next assembly meeting against the generals by introducing spurious mourners. But there is good reason to doubt the veracity of this story. For one thing, it is not supported by any other evidence. Diodorus mentions mourners appearing at the assembly meeting, but he does not attribute their appearance to Theramenes or suggest that they were illegitimate. And the claim that Theramenes suborned mourners does not appear elsewhere in our sources where we would most expect to find it were the story true—among the denunciations of Theramenes that appear in a law-court speech written by Lysias sometime after 403, and in Xenophon's own account of criticism heaped on Theramenes by a speaker in 404. On the face of it, moreover, the story is hard to believe. All it would have taken for the deception to be revealed during the assembly was for one of Theramenes' fake mourners to be recognized and outed by an acquaintance. Organizing such a fraud, therefore, and risking exposure as its instigator, would have been dangerous, and it arguably would have served little purpose: with some five thousand men dead at Arginusae, a good percentage of them Athenian citizens, there would surely have been no shortage of mourners in attendance anyway. Besides, as a number of scholars have pointed out, it wouldn't necessarily have been in Theramenes' interest to rile the Athenians, as their anger might well turn against the trierarchs rather than the generals.[17]

We can, I think, reject as unlikely Xenophon's claim that Theramenes arranged to have faux mourners infiltrate the assembly. That said, it was an unfortunate bit of luck that the Apaturia happened to fall during the proceedings against the generals. We can well imagine that the family reunions taking place across the city stoked the Athenians' sense of loss over the brothers and sons they'd sent off to die at Arginusae. Grief, in such circumstances, may well have morphed into anger at the men who'd failed to save their boys from drowning after the battle.

The Second Meeting of the Boule

Xenophon also claims that, during the Apaturia, Theramenes and his supporters "persuaded" one of the members of the boule, Callixenus, to accuse the generals at the council's next meeting. (The Greek word for *persuade* can also mean *bribe*, and it may have that meaning here.) We don't know whether Theramenes was in fact behind it, but Callixenus did address the boule when it met after the Apaturia, and he proposed a motion the other councilors voted on and passed. It would now be put to the assembly as the recommendation of the boule, and the Athenians would be free to ratify, reject, or amend it as they deemed fit.

Xenophon quotes the boule's proposal at length, but it can be summarized briefly:

1. The Athenians had heard the prosecution and defense arguments already in the first assembly, so the question of the general's guilt or innocence—whether or not they had "acted unjustly in not

picking up the men who had won the sea battle"—could now be put to a vote.

2. The Athenians would vote in the assembly by tribes, using ballots that would be dropped in one of two urns (one for acquittal, one for a guilty verdict). The generals would all be convicted or acquitted by the same vote.
3. If found guilty, the generals would be handed over to the Eleven for execution, and their property confiscated, with a tenth of the proceeds given to the goddess Athena.[18]

If the recommendation of the boule was accepted by the Athenians, in other words, the generals would not be given further opportunity to defend themselves. What they'd already said in relatively brief speeches delivered during the first assembly meeting—when they were unaware they were arguing for their lives—would have to suffice as their defense. Their guilt or innocence, moreover, would be determined at a different meeting than that in which their statements were heard. Since the second assembly would inevitably be attended by a different cross-section of the Athenian citizenry, some percentage of the men tasked with convicting or acquitting the generals would do so without having heard their arguments. The generals, Xenophon tells us, had been on the verge of winning the Athenians over at that first meeting, but they could not count on getting a comparable reception at the second assembly: not only had their audience changed, but popular sentiment may have turned against them in the interim due to the intervention of the Apaturia. If the Athenians approved the boule's proposal, then, the generals would find themselves in a very dangerous situation.

The Second Assembly Meeting

The opinion of the boule was introduced at the second assembly meeting, but it was not voted on at once. Indeed, much drama was to unfold before that vote occurred.

THE GUY ON THE BARLEY TUB

First, the assembly heard the report of a veteran of Arginusae, the man we mentioned earlier who claimed to have saved himself after the battle by clinging to a tub of barley. He told the assembly that the men who were in the water, "those who were dying," had tasked him with delivering a message to the

Athenian people if he made it through alive. He was "to report to the demos that the generals did not pick up the men who proved themselves best in service to their country." More than a century and a half ago George Grote waxed eloquent over this anonymous sailor's message: "I venture to say that there is nothing in the whole compass of ancient oratory, more full of genuine pathos and more profoundly impressive, than this simple incident and speech." Grote concludes that "there is nothing in the assertion of this man which is at all improbable," and perhaps he's right. But to my more cynical ear these alleged last words of drowning men seem at the least to have been gussied up for rhetorical effect. Or do men who are gasping their last really refer to themselves as those "who proved themselves best in service to their country"? I'm also skeptical that the incident took place—if it took place—as described. Xenophon's language suggests that the drowning men specifically selected the man on the meal tub to relay their message—they "tasked him" with the job (*epistellein*). Did they somehow recognize as he floated by that he was more likely to survive than they, and that he would thus be an effective messenger? The story seems fishy to me. My doubts aside, however, Grote is probably right that the man's speech packed an emotional wallop—or, as he puts it, "went to the inmost depth of the hearers' souls"—when delivered before an audience still raw from the losses sustained at Arginusae. Emotional testimony of the sort, of course, made it increasingly unlikely that the generals' future would be decided by a congenial audience.[19]

EURYPTOLEMUS'S *GRAPHE PARANOMON*

This was the atmosphere in the assembly when a man named Euryptolemus—a relative of Pericles and a friend of the general Diomedon—along with "some others," accused Callixenus of having drafted a proposal that was *paranomon*. This likely means that Euryptolemus initiated, or announced his intention to initiate, a procedure called a *graphe paranomon*, a suit alleging that a motion or decree was in violation of Athens' existing statutes or customary procedures—two possible meanings of the Greek word *nomos*. As we'll see below, Euryptolemus objected in particular to two aspects of Callixenus's proposal: that it called for the generals to be tried collectively, their guilt or innocence decided by a single vote, and that it would not allow the generals to defend themselves in a trial convened for the purpose. These same aspects likely trouble modern readers. But however disturbed we may be by Callixenus's motion, it seems likely that it was not illegal. In objecting to it, Euryptolemus does not point to any legislation that it supposedly contravened—or, at least, Xenophon hasn't recorded him doing so—nor did the Athenians have a constitution that guaranteed them the right to a fair trial. Rather than claiming that the motion transgressed existing law, then, Euryptolemus seems to have objected to it on the grounds that it violated customary practice: it was not the done thing in Athens, at least not usually, to condemn or acquit whole boards of magistrates by a single vote, nor to pass a verdict on men who had not had an adequate opportunity to defend themselves. Not the done thing, but not, strictly speaking, illegal. Whether legal or not, of course, Callixenus's motion offends our sense of fairness, which is why most readers probably come away from the Arginusae episode convinced that, whatever the legal niceties of the business, the generals got a raw deal.[20]

When a *graphe paranomon* was brought against a motion, the debate over the proposal would normally be adjourned until a court of law could render a verdict in the matter. Charging Callixenus with introducing a motion that was *paranomon*, then, should have led to a postponement of the discussion. But that's not what happened. While Euryptolemus had some support among the Athenians in attendance, Xenophon tells us, "the majority cried out that it would be terrible if someone did not allow the demos to do whatever it wanted." A man named Lysicus then suggested that if Euryptolemus and those who supported him didn't back down, they should be sentenced by the same vote as the generals. There was another outburst from the crowd, this time in support of Lysicus, and Euryptolemus and the others were compelled to withdraw their summons. The motion of Callixenus would not be preempted by a *graphe paranomon*.[21]

One gets the impression, reading Xenophon's account, that the Athenians responded to Euryptolemus's threat of a *graphe paranomon* by turning into an angry mob. When he's describing their reaction to Lysicus's threat, Xenophon refers to the Athenians as an *ochlos*—a word that can have the pejorative sense of "the mob." It's hard to tell from his text, however, whether things really were getting ugly in the assembly. The only action Xenophon attributes to the Athenian "mob" is disruptive speech. But outbursts from the audience were not unusual in Athens' assembly. Indeed, it has been argued that they were an integral feature of assembly debate. That the Athenians shouted and disrupted speakers during this meeting therefore does not imply that they were becoming moblike. One would very much like to have video of the meeting to see what the reality was. Angry mob or no, though, the Athenians weren't wrong in insisting that they should be free to do what they wanted: they were asserting the sovereignty of the demos in Athens' democracy, where, as Mark Munn writes, "the people's will *was* the law." It was their prerogative to decide the matter of the generals without reference to precedent, and to shout down those who, like Euryptolemus, attempted to thwart that process by appealing to technicalities.[22]

SOCRATES AND THE *PRYTANEIS*

The next obstacle to Callixenus's proposal being adopted came from the *prytaneis*, the tribal contingent of fifty men who were serving at the time as the executive committee of the boule. It was their job to preside over meetings of the assembly. A number of the *prytaneis* now refused to put the proposal to a vote "in violation of the law" (*para ton nomon*).[23] It may seem odd that the *prytaneis* objected at this point, since they would already have participated in the debate and vote on the proposal in the boule. But they may have taken issue with the motion earlier as well, or perhaps the discussion surrounding Euryptolemus's aborted *graphe paranomon* had altered their opinions.

Among the *prytaneis* who were now objecting was one of Athens' most famous citizens, the philosopher Socrates, who would have been in his sixties in 406, and some seven years away from answering to the Athenian people for his own purported crimes. It is an almost too-good-to-be-true coincidence that Socrates—who had never held another office in Athens throughout his long life—happened to serve in the boule in 406 and that his tribe happened to be in prytany when the Arginusae generals appeared before this second assembly. More coincidental yet, Socrates may have been serving as *epistates* on the day of the assembly, the one man selected by lot from the *prytaneis* to serve as chairman of the boule for the day—the closest thing Athens had to a head of state. Our sources, however, are not unanimous on this point. With Socrates and some number of the other *prytaneis* refusing to move forward with the decree, Callixenus rose to speak and "accused them of the same things," which seems to mean that, as Lysicus had earlier, he suggested the uncooperative *prytaneis* be sentenced by the same vote as the generals. The crowd cried out that those who refused to put the motion to a vote should be summoned to court. Now "terrified," Xenophon tells us, all of the *prytaneis* backed down, agreeing to put the motion to a vote, except for Socrates, who said that "he would do nothing except in accordance with *nomos*." Socrates' brave stance, however, ultimately came to nothing: he was evidently powerless, even if he was *epistates*, to prevent the matter from moving forward in the face of overwhelming popular support for a vote.[24]

EURYPTOLEMUS'S SPEECH

Callixenus's motion, however, was still not immediately put to a vote. Instead, Euryptolemus rose and addressed the assembly for a second time. By way of arguing that the generals had done nothing wrong, he spent part of his time telling the Athenians what had happened after the battle. It is from his speech, for example, that we learn about the division of responsibilities decided on by the Athenian command after they'd returned to Arginusae, information that Xenophon does not mention in his account of the battle and its aftermath. Euryptolemus's main point, however, is that it would be *para ton nomon*—a violation of the law or of traditional practice—for the Athenians to sentence the generals collectively and without a trial. He urges the Athenians instead to allow the generals to defend themselves in individual trials, and he mentions two laws under which they could be prosecuted: the decree of Cannonus and another law, which he does not name, that was used against traitors and temple robbers. Both of these procedures were at least as harsh as what Callixenus had proposed: under all three, a guilty verdict would result in the execution of the condemned and the confiscation of his property. The difference was that the laws Euryptolemus mentioned would allow the generals to defend themselves, the first before the demos and the second in court, while the decree of Callixenus would not. If the Athenians listened to him, Euryptolemus said, they would not be giving up their right to execute the generals should they find them guilty. They would, however, after hearing the generals' defense speeches, be better informed when they came to a decision, and they would have less cause for regret in the future. Euryptolemus closed his speech by formally proposing that the generals be tried under the decree of Cannonus.[25]

VOTE ON THE COMPETING PROPOSALS

Now that Euryptolemus had put forward a competing motion, a vote was held to determine whether the generals would be tried under the provisions of Callixenus's proposal or the decree of Cannonus, as Euryptolemus urged. The decision was by show of hands (*cheirotonia*), and it was the job of the *prytaneis* to determine which motion garnered the greater number of votes. When the decision was in, Euryptolemus's proposal had won the day: the generals, it seemed, would get their individual trials after all.

Or they would have, but a man named Menecles came forward and lodged an objection under oath. Xenophon doesn't tell us what the nature of his objection was, but it's likely that he questioned the *prytaneis*' assessment of the vote and demanded a recount—or a re-estimate, since hands raised in a vote conducted by *cheirotonia* were approximated rather than counted. Some of the *prytaneis*, remember, had objected to Callixenus's motion earlier in the day's proceedings, so it would not be surprising if their decision now in favor of Euryptolemus was viewed with suspicion. The result of Menecles' objection, at any rate, was that a second vote by show of hands was conducted. This time, Callixenus's motion was the winner.[26]

THE VERDICT

Once Euryptolemus's proposal had been voted down, there was no further obstacle to the implementation of Callixenus's motion, a collective vote on the generals' guilt or innocence. The procedure was conducted as Callixenus had proposed. Two urns were set up in the assembly for each tribe, and at each location a herald announced the ground rules: those who thought the generals "were guilty for not picking up the men who were victorious in the battle" were to cast their ballots in the first urn, while those who favored acquittal should use the second. This time, since the Athenians were not voting by *cheirotonia*, the assessment of the vote would be final.[27]

The ballots were thus cast and counted and, in the end, the news was grim: the defendants, the Athenians had decided, were guilty. Per the dictates of Callixenus's motion, the six generals who were in Athens were led off to be executed by the Eleven. According to Diodorus, however, one of the generals, Diomedon, paused first to ask a favor of the assembly. Before the battle, he explained, he and his colleagues had made vows to various gods in return for a victory. Since the generals were in no position now to pay what was promised, he asked that the Athenians do so on their behalf.[28]

The Fate of Callixenus

We can all agree, I'm sure, that the conclusion of the Arginusae business was lamentable. Six of Athens' generals, who had been responsible for a stunning naval victory against a technically superior fleet, were put to death by the Athenians for the loss of life that resulted from that battle, deaths that, so far as we can tell, could not have been prevented given the circumstances and were no fault of the generals or of anyone else. The Athenians themselves soon regretted what they had done. "Not much later," Xenophon writes, "the Athenians repented and resolved that complaints be brought against anyone who had deceived the people." Those who stood accused—and Callixenus, the assemblymen specified, was to be among them—were to furnish sureties, men who would guarantee their appearance at trial. Callixenus and four others were duly charged. Xenophon doesn't tell us who these others were, but we know that Theramenes was not one of them. It is tempting to identify Callixenus's fellow accused as those whom Xenophon mentions by name in his account of the Arginusae proceedings: Archedemus, who fined and prosecuted Erasinides; Timocrates, who moved at the first meeting of the boule that the generals be handed over to the assembly; Lysicus, who threatened Euryptolemus in connection with his proposed *graphe paranomon*; and Menecles, who objected to the *prytaneis*' assessment of the vote. But it is, of course, impossible to be sure about their identities.[29]

Xenophon and Diodorus disagree on the specifics of Callixenus's fate, but in neither case was it a happy one. According to Diodorus, Callixenus was tried without being allowed to defend himself, then bound and thrown into prison. He escaped with a number of others by digging his way out, and he ran off to Decelea, which was still occupied by the Spartans. Callixenus thus managed to escape death, Diodorus writes, but with the result that for the rest of his life the Greeks "pointed fingers of blame at his wickedness." As Xenophon tells the story, however, Callixenus's case never made it to trial. He and the other accused were kept in custody by their sureties—not by the state—pending their appearance in court, but they managed to escape from this private imprisonment sometime in 405, after the battle of Aegospotami. Callixenus eventually returned to Athens, after the general amnesty issued in 403 made it safe for him to do so, but "everyone hated him and he died of starvation."[30]

The Case against Theramenes

So much for Callixenus. It remains to consider the vexed question of Theramenes' culpability in the Arginusae debacle. Indeed, the trial of the generals was just one of several major historical events of the period in which Theramenes played a significant role. He was also involved in both of the short-lived oligarchic revolutions that ripped Athens apart in the last years of the fifth century. As one of the Four Hundred, the narrow oligarchy that came to power in Athens in 411, Theramenes eventually turned against his colleagues, advocating the replacement of their regime by a broader group, the Five Thousand. Because of his support for a more democratic government, Theramenes remained in favor when the democracy was restored in 410, but he gained a reputation in the process as an opportunist who was adept at political survival. Theramenes' later involvement with the Thirty Tyrants, however, the oligarchy that was imposed on the Athenians after they lost the war with Sparta in 404, led ultimately to his execution—one of the more dramatic deaths known to us from antiquity. Theramenes was ripped from an altar in the boule at which he'd been seeking sanctuary. Dragged through the streets screaming of his mistreatment, he was later forced to drink hemlock, a quaff he prefaced with a toast to the man responsible for his execution. Theramenes was a controversial figure in his own time, loathed by some of his contemporaries and loved by others, and modern scholars have inherited the debate over his character and slippery loyalties. Happily, we need not decide for ourselves what sort of a man Theramenes was overall, but we ought to come to some conclusion about his behavior during the Arginusae proceedings.[31]

As we've seen, Xenophon portrays Theramenes as the bad guy in his account of the Arginusae episode: Theramenes accuses the generals at the first meeting of the assembly, organizes fake mourners to infiltrate the next meeting, and induces Callixenus to bring forward his infamous motion in the boule. We've discussed these events already, but I'd like to revisit them briefly with a view to rendering a final verdict on Theramenes' conduct.

First, as Xenophon tells the story, Theramenes attacked the generals at the first meeting of the assembly without provocation. But there is reason to doubt the spin he puts on things. As we've seen, Theramenes' mention of the generals' first letter during that meeting doesn't fit in the context of an attack. Theramenes appears instead to be defending himself against accusations implicit in the generals' second batch of letters. Nor does Theramenes appear to have gone after the generals very aggressively at the meeting. From what Xenophon tells us, the thrust of his speech seems to have been that the generals should be made "to render an account" for not picking up the shipwrecked sailors. We said above that Xenophon's language here suggests Theramenes was referring to an *euthyna*. If that is correct, then he was calling for the generals to undergo a procedure to which they would have been subjected anyway as a matter of course. Theramenes thus appears to have been treading a careful line at the assembly meeting, saying enough to defend himself while not escalating the hostilities. For their part, the generals appear to have responded in kind. They reiterated that the trierarchs had been given the job of rescuing the shipwrecked, but they refused to blame anything but the storm for the failure of that mission.[32]

Xenophon further claims that during the celebration of the Apaturia, Theramenes suborned mourners to appear at the second assembly meeting. I've argued above that the story is unlikely to be true. At the most we might believe that Theramenes induced legitimate mourners to attend the assembly, but this too seems unlikely, since riling up the demos over the Arginusae issue could easily have backfired on Theramenes.[33]

Finally, Theramenes reportedly "persuaded" Callixenus—which may mean that he bribed him—to propose his infamous motion in the boule. We can't know whether Theramenes was behind Callixenus's proposal or not, but I agree with Donald Kagan that the accusation is "implausible and unnecessary": "Callixenus's proposal would have been of no value if more than half of the five hundred members of the council had not approved it. If so many men liked the idea, why was there need to bribe someone to put it forth?"[34]

If we look closely at Theramenes' alleged misdeeds, then, the case against him begins to fall apart. Certainly he does not appear to be the blackguard Xenophon portrays him as, inexplicably intent upon destroying the generals he had served under at Arginusae. That Theramenes was never charged in connection with the Arginusae proceedings, even though the Athenians were aggressive in pursuing Callixenus and a number of others, makes the case against him weaker yet. The prosecution, I suggest, has not met its burden of proof: with regard to the Arginusae affair, at least, Theramenes should be acquitted of wrongdoing.[35]

The Culpability of the Demos

It is more difficult to acquit the Athenian people. Ironically, it's also difficult to convict them of any particular offense. As we've discussed above, there doesn't seem to have been anything illegal about the trial of the generals. Xenophon's report that the generals spoke only briefly at the first assembly meeting because "a speech was not permitted them in accordance with the law"[36] has been taken by some as evidence of illegality, but Xenophon's wording is ambiguous and doesn't necessarily support that conclusion. Callixenus's motion, too, was opposed by Euryptolemus and Socrates, among others, on the grounds that it was *paranomon*, but as we've seen, the meaning of that word is slippery, and Euryptolemus, at least, seems to have objected to the proposal because it contravened customary practices rather than any standing statutes.

If the Athenians can't be blamed for conducting an illegal trial, perhaps we can fault them instead for condemning the generals in a fit of rage. One gets the impression from Xenophon's account, after all, that the Athenians turned into an ugly mob at the second assembly meeting, stifling opposition to Callixenus's motion with cries that the demos should be free to do what it wanted.

But a closer look at what happened at the meeting suggests that this view of the assemblymen is erroneous. The Athenians responded to Euryptolemus's proposed *graphe paranomon* and the intransigence of the *prytaneis* with speech, outbursts that signaled their opposition to or support of various speakers. Disruptions of the sort were a staple of Athenian democratic debate, however, and thus not evidence in themselves that the crowd was out of control. Having opposed Euryptolemus's *graphe paranomon*, moreover, the Athenians subsequently allowed him to speak in the generals' defense, at considerable length and apparently without significant interruption—hardly the behavior of an enraged mob. Words were hurled in the assembly, it is true, but nothing more: there was no threat of violence. The closest the Athenians came to making threats was when they voiced their support of those suggesting Euryptolemus and the *prytaneis* be sentenced by the same vote as the generals. In this the Athenians arguably committed a moral wrong.

The Athenians also cannot be accused of a precipitous rush to judgment in the case of the generals. Their trial—which was not a trial at all, really, but a series of related proceedings—was a lengthy and complicated business that stretched across multiple days: there were two meetings of the assembly, two meetings of the boule, multiple votes taken, numerous speeches heard on both sides, and alternative modes of prosecution considered. The Athenians ultimately opted to forego a traditional trial, but it was not because they were looking to finish the job as quickly as possible: trying the generals in accordance with the motion of Callixenus was, for whatever reason and however unfair it seems to us, the Athenians' considered preference.

We are left with the perhaps uncomfortable conclusion that the Athenians, with due consideration and in accordance with all standing statutes, reached a verdict in the Arginusae affair that was perfectly legal but at the same time perfectly reprehensible. The Athenians themselves soon came to believe that their condemnation of the generals had been wrong. They blamed Callixenus and a handful of other speakers for having "deceived" them in the matter. No one, of course, had forced the Athenians to cast their ballots as they had, but the demos, unlike the hundreds of magistrates who held office in Athens annually, could not be held to account for its decisions. Instead, those who urged Athens' assemblymen to make decisions they later regretted often paid a price for their persuasiveness. Callixenus, the villain of our story, got his comeuppance during his lifetime. But the Athenians, by executing their victorious generals after Arginusae, earned a reputation for mob rule and self-destructive irrationality that would outlast their radical democracy by millennia.

Epilogue

THE WAR WAS SOON OVER. In the summer of 405 the Spartans annihilated Athens' fleet in a single stroke, in a battle off of Aegospotami, on the north shore of the Hellespont. After several days of refusing to put to sea when the Athenians lined up for battle against them, the Spartans pounced when their enemy was unprepared—with most of their ships unmanned or only partially manned, many of the men themselves having gone off to procure provisions. The Spartans captured 171 of the Athenians' 180 ships, along with several thousand sailors, all of whom were subsequently executed. News of the debacle was brought to Athens by the Paralus, one of the handful of triremes that had escaped capture. Xenophon's description of the ship's arrival in Athens is one of the more affecting passages in his history:

> The Paralus arrived in Athens during the night with news of the disaster, and a wailing spread from the Piraeus up the Long Walls to the city, one man telling another, so that that night no one slept.

The next morning the Athenians met in assembly. There was no question any longer of their meeting the Peloponnesians at sea, but neither were they ready to surrender—an act that they feared would entail the destruction of their city and the execution or enslavement of its citizens. They resolved instead to prepare for a siege.[1]

The Spartans, for their part, were soon investing Athens by land and sea, and in particular preventing merchant ships from delivering grain to the city. The Athenians withstood the deprivations that resulted for some time, but when the people began to starve to death, and after many months spent negotiating terms with the Spartans (talks in which our old friend Theramenes was deeply, and controversially, involved), they finally surrendered in March or April of 404—just over twenty-seven years after the war had begun. The Spartans, to their great credit, were magnanimous in victory. Athens' population was allowed to live, and the city itself was not destroyed but only hobbled: the Spartans required that the Athenians surrender all but twelve of their ships and that the Long Walls and the walls of the Piraeus be demolished. After the agreement was struck, the Spartans sailed into the Piraeus, Xenophon tells us, and "with great zeal began tearing down the walls to the music of flute-girls, thinking that that day was the beginning of freedom for Greece."[2]

When the Peloponnesian War began in 431, the Greek world was divided into two blocs. Athens and Sparta, the two superpowers of the day, enjoyed military dominance in different spheres: the Spartans were preeminent on land, while the Athenians were the recognized masters of the sea. The Spartans ultimately won the war because they managed to develop a navy that was capable of beating the Athenians at their own game. But even so they could not have won had they not had the support of a succession of Persian grandees—including Pharnabazus, who financed the construction of a new Peloponnesian fleet after the Spartans lost everything at Cyzicus. The Athenians, on the other hand, did not have the resources needed to continually build and man new fleets. As long as the Persians were willing to bankroll the Spartans, then, the Athenians simply could not have prevailed in the war, however many talented military leaders they may have had at their disposal: their execution of the six Arginusae generals, therefore, ultimately made no difference to the war's outcome.

As I suggested at the end of chapter 5, however, the Athenians' execution of the generals did leave a mark. The Athenians caught flack in antiquity from writers who saw in the Arginusae trial evidence of the deficiencies of popular rule. And they were routinely castigated by seventeenth- and eighteenth-century historians for their irrationality and inconstancy, with the Arginusae proceedings chief among detractors' complaints. Sir Walter Raleigh, for example, writing in the early seventeenth century, concluded that the abuses the Athenians suffered under the Thirty Tyrants, the cruel oligarchy imposed on the city after the war, were divine retribution inflicted on the "rascal multitude" for the "infamy of injustice" of the generals' executions. Charles Rollin, who wrote his twelve-volume *Ancient History* in the first half of the eighteenth century, numbered the Arginusae trial among the worst abuses committed by the fickle Athenian demos:

> "The people of Athens," says Plutarch, "were easily provoked to anger, and as easily induced to resume their sentiments of benevolence and compassion." History supplies us with an infinity of examples of this kind. The sentence of death passed against the inhabitants of Mytilene, and revoked the next day: the condemnation of the ten generals, and that of Socrates, both followed with an immediate repentance and the most lively grief.

Earlier in his history, in his account of the Arginusae episode, Rollin agrees with the author of the Socratic dialogue *Axiochus* that the demos "is an inconstant, ungrateful, cruel, suspicious animal, incapable of submitting to the government of reason, which is no wonder . . . as it is commonly composed of the dregs of a city, and is a monstrous assemblage, without form or order, of all that is worst in it." Later in the eighteenth century William Mitford contended in his *History of Greece* that the victory at Arginusae "might have gone far to procure final success to Athens, had Athens had a government capable of any steadiness, or even secure against acts of madness." He refers to the Arginusae proceedings as "one of the most extraordinary, most disgraceful, and most fatal strokes of faction recorded in history." Such depictions of Athens' democracy were influential in their day and likely influenced in particular the founding fathers of the United States, who "recoiled with force from the Athenian example and from the notion of direct democracy with which it was inextricably associated," modeling their new polity instead on the mixed constitution of the Roman Republic.[3]

Modern historians are likewise wont to portray the Arginusae proceedings as an example of "mob rule" or "mob terrorism," the "moral nadir of democracy."[4] Seeing evidence of the failings of Athens' government in the Arginusae affair thus has a long history. I've suggested above, however, that the verdict in the Arginusae trial was in fact a product of deliberate consideration rather than of rash action. The outbursts from the assemblymen that Xenophon records—which to many readers have understandably sounded like the ravings of an enraged mob—were not unusual or unexpected in the context of Athenian political debate. Xenophon's account of the proceedings, therefore, should not be viewed as a devastating indictment of Athens' democracy. But while the Athenians may not have tried the generals illegally and in a fit of rage, as many have supposed, it remains true that something went wrong in the course of the proceedings, since the verdict appears to us, and seems to have appeared to the Athenians as well, as a travesty of justice.

So what went wrong? I believe that in holding the generals to blame for the losses sustained at Arginusae the Athenians, simply put, made a terrible mistake. Unfortunately, unlike their resolution twenty-one years earlier to execute all the male citizens of Mytilene, this decision was irrevocable, since the penalty required by their verdict was quickly imposed. But bad decisions are by no means peculiar to direct democracies: that the Arginusae affair ended as it did does not imply that the political system under which the guilty verdict was handed down was debased or irrational or unworkable. Of the "infinity of examples" Charles Rollin claimed as evidence for Plutarch's view of the fickle Athenian mob, he cites only three: Mytilene, Arginusae, and the execution of Socrates, a familiar triumvirate of black marks routinely mentioned in discussions of the follies of Athens' democracy. But against these exceptional cases stand the hundred-odd years before Socrates' trial, during which the Athenians arguably governed themselves and, eventually, their empire well. Had the Athenian demos of the fifth century really been a crazed, irrational mob, Athens likely would not have achieved the success it did, and the Athenians would probably have lost the war with Sparta much sooner than they did. The Athenian democracy was an outstanding accomplishment, an experiment in popular rule, forged in the wake of tyrannical oppression, that ushered in an era of unprecedented artistic, literary, and intellectual accomplishment. That the Athenians sometimes made mistakes—the Arginusae verdict among them—does not negate that achievement.

APPENDIX A

Sequence of Events from the Storm to the Deposition of the Generals

For a full discussion of these events, see pages 53–57 and 75–86.

A storm prevents the Athenians from sailing to Mytilene and mounting a rescue and recovery operation immediately after the battle (Xenophon, *Hellenica* 1.6.35; Diodorus 13.100.2–3). After the storm, Eteonicus leaves Mytilene, ending the blockade of Conon (Xenophon, *Hellenica* 1.6.36–38; Diodorus 13.100.5).

Conon leaves Mytilene. The Athenian fleet (all but forty-seven ships) sails from Arginusae toward Mytilene and meets Conon's fleet en route (Xenophon, *Hellenica* 1.6.38; Diodorus 13.100.6). Meanwhile, the forty-seven ships under Theramenes and Thrasybulus begin their rescue and recovery operation.

The generals send a letter to the demos and boule reporting on the battle and "blaming nothing other than the storm" (Xenophon, *Hellenica* 1.7.4; cf. Diodorus 13.101.1). They do not mention the role of the trierarchs (Xenophon, *Hellenica* 1.7.17).

The main Athenian fleet sails against Chios and then to Samos (Xenophon, *Hellenica* 1.6.38; Diodorus 13.100.6).

The generals' letter arrives in Athens.

The rescue ships (some of them, at least) rendezvous with the rest of the fleet at Samos. Theramenes and Thrasybulus return to Athens before the rest of the fleet (Diodorus 13.101.2) with the remains of the dead.

The generals at Arginusae hear that the mood in Athens is turning against them. They assume that the trierarchs are slandering them (Diodorus 13.101.2).

The generals send letters to the demos saying they had ordered the trierarchs to recover the dead (Diodorus 13.101.2).

The letters are read in the assembly. The trierarchs successfully defend themselves (Diodorus 13.101.4).

The Athenians vote to depose and recall the generals (Xenophon, *Hellenica* 1.7.1; Diodorus 13.101.5), probably in early to mid-September (see chap. 5, note 1).

APPENDIX B

Sequence of Events after the Generals' Return to Athens

For a full discussion of these events, see pages 75–86.

Archedemus fines Erasinides (Xenophon, *Hellenica* 1.7.2).

Archedemus accuses Erasinides in a law court (1) of embezzlement and (2) "concerning his generalship." Erasinides is imprisoned (Xenophon, *Hellenica* 1.7.2), probably as a debtor to the state.

The generals report to the boule, which imprisons them and hands them over to the assembly (Xenophon, *Hellenica* 1.7.3).

Theramenes, the generals, and numerous others address the assembly, which ultimately orders the boule to draft a proposal regarding how the generals should be tried (Xenophon, *Hellenica* 1.7.4–7).

The Apaturia is celebrated (Xenophon, *Hellenica* 1.7.8) on three consecutive days sometime between October 9 and October 23 (see chap. 5, note 16).

The boule meets for the second time (in mid to late October: see chap. 5, note 16) and approves Callixenus's proposal (Xenophon, *Hellenica* 1.7.9–10), which would then be put to the assembly.

The assembly meets for the second time.

- The boule introduces its proposal (Xenophon, *Hellenica* 1.7.9–10).
- A veteran of Arginusae addresses the assembly (Xenophon, *Hellenica* 1.7.11).
- Euryptolemus and others accuse Callixenus of introducing an illegal proposal but are forced to withdraw the summons (Xenophon, *Hellenica* 1.7.12–13).
- Some of the *prytaneis* (including Socrates) object to putting the proposal to a vote. After Callixenus threatens them, all but Socrates back down (Xenophon, *Hellenica* 1.7.14–15; cf. Plato, *Apology* 32b).
- Euryptolemus addresses the assembly, proposing that the generals be tried under the provisions of the decree of Cannonus (Xenophon, *Hellenica* 1.7.16–34).
- In a vote by show of hands, the Athenians decide to try the generals in accordance with the decree of Cannonus (Xenophon, *Hellenica* 1.7.34).
- Menecles objects under oath to the vote. (Xenophon, *Hellenica* 1.7.34).

- In a second show of hands, the Athenians decide to try the generals in accordance with Callixenus's motion (Xenophon, *Hellenica* 1.7.34).
- In a vote by ballot, the Athenians convict the eight generals who had commanded at Arginusae (Xenophon, *Hellenica* 1.7.34).
- Diomedon addresses the assembly regarding vows the generals made prior to the battle (Diodorus 13.102.1–3).

The six generals who are in Athens are executed (Xenophon, *Hellenica* 1.7.34; Diodorus 13.102.4).

NOTES

Prologue

1. Seventy-two-degree water: This is an estimate for the water temperature of the North Aegean at the time of the Battle of Arginusae. In 1991 and 1992 the surface temperature of the Aegean during the summer ranged from 21° to 26°C (69.8° to 78.8°F): D. Yagar, "Late glacial-Holocene evolution of the Aegean Sea" (Ph.D. diss., Institute of Marine Sciences and Technology, Dokuz Eylül University, 1994), cited at http://www.newworldencyclopedia.org/entry/Aegean_Sea. See also Şeniz Uçkaç, "Sea Surface Variability in the Aegean Sea," *E.U. Journal of Fisheries & Aquatic Sciences* 22 (2005): 130. The highest temperature recorded in the North Aegean in the summers of 1987, 1991, and 1994 was 23.5°C (74.3°F). For expected survival times in cold water see http://www.ussartf.org/cold_water_survival.htm. Sites last accessed 9/13/2012.

2. Diodorus 13.98.5. Thucydides similarly says that the Battle of Sybota in 433 was greater than any other fought between Greeks to that time in terms of the number of vessels engaged (260): 1.46.1, 1.47.1, 1.50.2.

Chapter I: Setting the Stage: From Xerxes' Invasion to the Eve of Arginusae

1. Herodotus 7.57.1.

2. For the relative sizes of the Persian and Roman Empires, see http://en.wikipedia.org/wiki/List_of_largest_empires (last accessed 3/8/2014).

3. "Single most important human fact": Paul Cartledge, *The Spartans: The World of the Warrior-Heroes of Ancient Greece* (New York: Vintage Books, 2003), 29. *Krypteia* is derived from the adjective *kryptos*, meaning "secret." "Time in hiding" is J. E. Lendon's translation of the term: *Song of Wrath: The Peloponnesian War Begins* (New York: Basic Books, 2010), 32. Policing and training: Athenaeus 657d; Plato, *Laws* 633b; Plutarch, *Lycurgus* 28.

4. Always on their guard: Thucydides 4.80.3, 5.23.3; Aristotle, *Politics* 1269a37–39. Forbidden from other work: Plutarch, *Lycurgus* 24. Toughened up: Plutarch, *Lycurgus* 16–18. In addition to the helots, *perioikoi*, and Spartiates, the Spartan state was populated by two other groups. The *hypomeiones* ("inferiors"; Xenophon, *Hellenica* 3.3.6) are thought to have been Spartans who, for one reason or another, had been excluded from full citizenship. *Mothakes*, meanwhile, may have been impoverished *hypomeiones* who were adopted by a wealthier family and put through the *agoge*. When I refer to Spartan armies or fleets in this book as "the Spartans," readers should understand that this is shorthand

for Spartan-led forces that might include any combination of Peloponnesian League members, helots, ex-helots, mercenaries, *perioikoi*, Spartiates, *hypomeiones*, and *mothakes*.

5. Spartan ships at Salamis: Herodotus 8.43. Conquer or die: Herodotus 7.104.5.

6. Persian invasion and Battle of Marathon: Herodotus 6.94–120. At least two to one: The Persians may have had about 25,000 fighting men at Marathon against roughly 10,000 Athenians. The Plataeans, the only Greeks to help the Athenians, added perhaps a thousand more. See N. G. L. Hammond, "The Campaign and Battle of Marathon," *Journal of Hellenic Studies* 88 (1968): 34.

7. Themistocles and the construction of the fleet: *Athenaion Politeia* 22.7; Herodotus 7.144.1; Thucydides 1.14.3. Two hundred ships: Herodotus 8.61.2.

8. Nearly half the ships in the allied fleet: Herodotus 8.43–48. The Athenians had 180 ships at Salamis out of a total of 368 in the Greek fleet. Execution of the Persian governor: Herodotus 9.120.4.

9. Spartans command by land and sea: Herodotus 8.2.2. Pausanias and the transfer of leadership: *Athenaion Politeia* 23.4; Herodotus 8.3.2; Plutarch, *Aristides* 23; Thucydides 1.94–95. However graceful their exit, the Spartans—or some Spartans—may not have been happy about the transfer of authority to Athens: *Athenaion Politeia* 23.2; Diodorus 11.50.

10. Oaths: *Athenaion Politeia* 23.5. Delos: Thucydides 1.96.

11. Quiescence: It might have shared the fate of the Hellenic League, which was not formally dissolved after the Greek victories over Persia in 480 and 479: Thucydides 1.102.4. "Autonomous allies": Thucydides 1.97.1. Pericles: Thucydides 2.63.2.

12. Athenians in violation of Peace: Thucydides 1.87.1–3, 1.125. Corcyra: Thucydides 1.46–54. Potidaea: Thucydides 1.56–65. Spartans attempt to provoke a confrontation: Thucydides 2.11.6, 2.18–20. Athenian anger over invasion: Thucydides 2.21.2–3. The Athenians, however, did send out cavalry to harass the Spartan troops: Thucydides 2.19, 2.22.2, 3.1.2. Raiding expeditions: Thucydides 2.23.2, 2.25, 2.30; cf. 2.56.1–2, 3.16.2, 3.94.1.

13. City and Piraeus walls: Thucydides 1.89.3–91, 1.93.3. Long Walls: Thucydides 1.107.1, 1.108.3. Middle wall: *Archaic Times to the End of the Peloponnesian War: Translated Documents of Greece and Rome*, ed. and trans. Charles W. Fornara (Baltimore: Johns Hopkins University Press, 1977), no. 79. Athens as island: Thucydides 1.143.5.

14. "Enormous and squalid refugee camp": Hanson, *War Like No Other* (New York: Random House, 2005), 45, cf. 68; Thucydides 2.17. Thucydides' discussion of the plague at 2.47–54 is well worth the read, particularly since he contracted the disease himself and survived.

15. Spartan invasions: In *431*: Thucydides 2.18–20, 2.23; *430*: 2.47.2, 2.55, 2.57; *429*: 2.71 (the Spartans marched against Plataea in Boeotia rather than Attica); *428*: 3.1; *427*: 3.26; *426*: 3.89.1 (invasion aborted due to earthquake); *425*: 4.2.1, 4.6. The longest invasion was the second, which lasted forty days: Thucydides 2.57.2. The invasion of 425 lasted only fifteen days: Thucydides 4.6.2. Natural disasters: In the 460s, an earthquake in the Peloponnese had precipitated a helot revolt (Thucydides 1.101.2). The helots, Aristotle writes at *Politics* 1269a37–39, were always sitting in wait for some such disaster to befall the Spartans.

16. Enterprising general: More accurately, he was general elect. His command would officially start in midsummer: Charles W. Fornara, *The Athenian Board of Generals from 501 to 404* (Wiesbaden: Franz Steiner Verlag, 1971), 57. Rebellious helots: Thucydides

4.80.2. "Die with them in their hands": Thucydides 4.40.1. Pylos and Sphacteria: Thucydides 4.2.4–4.6.1, 4.8–15, 4.23, 4.26–39, 4.41.1, 5.15.1.

17. Athenian demands: Thucydides 4.41.3–4. Delium: Thucydides 4.76, 4.90–100. Amphipolis: Thucydides 4.102–106, 4.108.1. Thucydides, the author of the *History of the Peloponnesian War*, was serving as a general in the north at the time and was held responsible for the loss of Amphipolis, as he failed to arrive in time to prevent the Amphipolitans from capitulating to the Spartans. He was in exile afterwards for twenty years (Thucydides 5.26.5).

18. Peace of Nicias: Thucydides 5.15–25.

19. Ten Years' War: Thucydides 5.25.1. Ironic nomenclature: G. E. M. de Ste. Croix, *Origins of the Peloponnesian War* (London: Duckworth, 1972), 294–295. Archidamus's speech: Thucydides 1.80–85.

20. Refusal of Spartan allies: Thucydides 5.17.2, 5.22.1. Failure to return Amphipolis: Thucydides 5.21, 5.35.5. Failure to return Pylos: Thucydides 5.35.4–7. Almost seven years: Thucydides 5.25.3. Athenian raids: Thucydides 6.105.2. Helots at Pylos: Thucydides 5.56.2, 5.115.2. Battle of Mantinea: Thucydides 5.64–75. The Spartans ultimately recaptured Pylos in the winter of 409/8: Xenophon, *Hellenica* 1.2.18.

21. Egesta requests help: Thucydides 6.6.2. Grain supply: Peter Green, *Armada from Athens* (New York: Doubleday, 1970), 16–19. Most splendid force: Thucydides 6.31. The Athenians had dispatched fleets this large before, but those were operating closer to home and were not as well provisioned. Athenians send more men and ships: Thucydides 6.94.4, 6.98.1, 7.16.2, 7.20.2, 7.42.1.

22. The Athenian general Nicias, at least, did recognize that the Sicilian Expedition was a mistake: Thucydides 6.10.1–4. The Spartans go to Sicily: Thucydides 6.73.2, 6.93, 6.104.1, 7.2.4, 7.21.

23. Thucydides 7.19.1–2, 7.27–28. The Spartans had been toying with the idea of fortifying Decelea since the winter of 415/14, when the Athenian traitor Alcibiades suggested the strategy to them (Thucydides 6.91.6, 6.93.1–2). The Spartans were also buoyed by the thought that the Athenians had patently broken the peace in the summer of 414 by making raids on the Spartan territory of Laconia itself, which they had been careful not to do previously (6.105.1–2, 7.18.3).

24. Loss of men and ships in Sicily: Thucydides 7.74.2, 7.85–87. Demosthenes, who had fortified Pylos back in 425, was also executed by the Syracusans.

25. Treasury depleted: Thucydides 8.4, 8.15.1, 8.53.2. Desertions: Thucydides 7.27.5. Allies ripe for revolt: Thucydides 8.2.2.

26. Intrigues with Sparta: Thucydides 8.5–6. Rebellions: Thucydides 8.14.2–3, 8.17.2–3, 8.19.4, 8.22.2, 8.35.1, 8.44. Sixty ships: Thucydides 8.6.4. Chios was one of only two allies in the Delian League that had still been contributing ships rather than money to Athens: Thucydides 6.85.2. (Methymna on Lesbos was the other. It likewise revolted in 412 but was quickly brought to heel by the Athenians: Thucydides 1.19.1, 3.10.5.)

27. Two-part plan: Thucydides 8.8.2. Underestimated Athenians' ability: Thucydides 8.24.5. About a hundred ships: By the end of the summer of 412 the Athenians had sent out ninety-four ships: see A. W. Gomme, A. Andrewes, and K. J. Dover, *A Historical Commentary on Thucydides*, vol. 5 (Oxford: Clarendon Press, 1981), 27–28, §§ 2 and 6. In the summer of 411 the Spartans and their allies had 110 ships in the Aegean against 108 Athenian ships: Thucydides 8.79.

28. Thucydides 8.5.4–5, 8.6.1, 8.80.2.

29. Insufficient pay: Thucydides 8.29, 8.37.4, 8.45.2, 8.58.5, 8.78, 8.83.2. Phoenician fleet: Thucydides 8.46, 8.78, 8.87.3. Pharnabazus ready to pay: Thucydides 8.80.2. Raising rebellions: Thucydides 8.61.1, 8.62, 8.80.1–3, 8.99. Eighty-six ships: Thucydides 8.103.1.

30. Cynossema: Thucydides 8.104–106; Diodorus 13.39–40. Abydus: Xenophon, *Hellenica* 1.2–7; Diodorus 13.45–47.2. Cyzicus: Xenophon, *Hellenica* 1.1.16–25; Diodorus 13.49.2–52.1. Thucydides' *History* ends abruptly shortly after his discussion of Cynossema. His account of the war is taken up by the contemporary historian Xenophon in his *Hellenica*, which covers the years from 411 to 362. Xenophon's history—which is much inferior to that of his predecessor—can be supplemented by the accounts of Diodorus and Plutarch, who wrote in the first century B.C. and the first century A.D., respectively.

31. Xenophon, *Hellenica* 1.4.9–10; Diodorus 13.68.1–2.

32. Eighty ships at Samos: Xenophon, *Hellenica* 1.4.21–23, 1.5.18. Ninety ships at Ephesus: Xenophon, *Hellenica* 1.5.1, 1.5.10.

33. Xenophon, *Hellenica* 1.4.3, 1.5.1–7.

34. Xenophon, *Hellenica* 1.5.10–17; *Hellenica Oxyrhynchia* 4.3; Diodorus 13.71; Plutarch, *Alcibiades* 35, *Lysander* 5.

35. Xenophon, *Hellenica* 1.5.16–17.

36. One hundred forty ships: Xenophon, *Hellenica* 1.6.3. Seventy ships manned: Xenophon, *Hellenica* 1.5.20; Diodorus 13.77.1–2. The Athenians presumably could have manned at least a dozen more, since Diomedon later showed up at Mytilene with twelve ships: see note 40. Attack on Methymna: Xenophon, *Hellenica* 1.6.12–13; Diodorus 13.76.5. Conon, Leon, Archestratus, and Erasinides: Xenophon, *Hellenica* 1.6.16; Lysias 21.8.

37. Arginusae: Diodorus 13.77.1–2. Callicratidas's message: Xenophon, *Hellenica* 1.6.15; Debra Hamel, *Trying Neaira: The True Story of a Courtesan's Scandalous Life in Ancient Greece* (New Haven: Yale University Press, 2003), 68.

38. The pursuit and battle: Xenophon, *Hellenica* 1.6.16–18; Diodorus 13.77.2–78.3. We know that Archestratus died at Mytilene (Lysias 21.8). It seems likely that it was during this battle in the harbor. Xenophon, *Hellenica* 1.6.16 implies, at any rate, that Archestratus never made it into Mytilene.

39. Xenophon, *Hellenica* 1.6.26.

40. Xenophon, *Hellenica* 1.6.19–22. Erasinides' later participation in the Battle of Arginusae implies that he escaped from Mytilene: Xenophon, *Hellenica* 1.6.29. Leon seems to have been commanding: W. James. McCoy, "The Identity of Leon," *American Journal of Philology* 96 (1975): 193. After the one ship escaped, the Athenian general Diomedon came to Mytilene, presumably from Samos, with a fleet of twelve ships. Callicratidas defeated this squadron, taking ten vessels. Diomedon escaped with his own and one other ship: Xenophon, *Hellenica* 1.6.22–23. It's tempting to think that the trireme that escaped from Mytilene somehow got word to Samos about the blockade, prompting Diomedon's ill-fated attempt to help.

Chapter II: Naval Warfare: Ramming, Dying, and Breaking Wind at Sea

1. Trireme crew: J. S. Morrison, J. F. Coates, and N. B. Rankov, *The Athenian Trireme: The History and Reconstruction of an Ancient Greek Warship*, 2nd ed. (Cambridge: Cambridge University Press, 2000), 107–113, 257. A trireme could carry more fighting men if

the hoplites doubled as rowers. This was sometimes done (Thucydides 3.18.4), but it was not standard practice, probably because the crew of a trireme needed to be highly trained if it was to perform well in battle. Ships could also be modified to carry more soldiers: Plutarch, *Cimon* 12.

2. Trireme speed: Morrison et al., *Athenian Trireme*, xxvii, 102–106.

3. Maintenance: Thucydides 7.12.4.

4. "Slept and rowed by turns": Thucydides 3.49.3. Going ashore for meals: Thucydides 8.95.4, 8.101; Xenophon, *Hellenica* 6.2.30.

5. Precautions against attack: Xenophon, *Hellenica* 6.2.29. Mealtime attacks: Thucydides 7.39–40.3, 8.95.4–5; Xenophon, *Hellenica* 2.1.22–28.

6. Oars under water: Morrison et al., *Athenian Trireme*, 248. If a ship heeled significantly in the wind, water could seep in through the thalamian oarports (261).

7. Storm off Mount Athos: Herodotus 6.44. Pair of storms: Herodotus 7.188–191, 8.13. Pylos: Thucydides 4.3–4. Triremes in bad weather: Thucydides 2.84.3, 8.31.3, 8.80.3; Herodotus 8.13; Diodorus 13.41.1–3, 13.46.4, 13.64.6.

8. Athlit ram: http://www.hms.org.il/Museum/Templates/showpage.asp?DBID=1&LNGID=1&TMID=84&FID=1196&PID=2949 (last accessed 3/8/2014). A number of smaller rams have been found in recent years off the western coast of Sicily, at the site of the Battle of the Aegates Islands, which was fought between the Romans and Carthaginians in 241 BC. See, e.g.: http://archaeologynewsnetwork.blogspot.com/2013/04/rare-bronze-rams-found-at-site-of-final.html (last accessed 3/8/2014). Naval inventories: *Inscriptiones Graecae* II^2 1604–32. Zea ship-sheds: J. S. Morrison and R. T. Williams, *Greek Oared Ships, 900–322 B.C.* (Cambridge: Cambridge University Press, 1968), 181–192.

9. Morrison et al., *Athenian Trireme*, xvii-xxviii.

10. Morrison et al., *Athenian Trireme*, 266; Timothy Shaw, "Is Olympias a Trieres?," in *The Trireme Project: Operational Experience, 1987–90, Lessons Learnt*, ed. Timothy Shaw (Oxford: Oxbow Books, 1993), 106; Frank Welsh, *Building the Trireme* (London: Constable, 1988), 80–82. Based on skeletal remains, the average height of an ancient Greek male is estimated to have been about 5′5″ (168 cm) versus about 5′7″ today (175 cm).

11. For the etymology of *thranitae*, see J. S. Morrison, "Notes on Certain Greek Nautical Terms and on Three Passages in I.G. ii^2. 1632," *Classical Quarterly* 41 (1947): 129–130.

12. Morrison et al., *Athenian Trireme*, 238. With all the sweating that was going on, the rowers felt "relatively little need to urinate," despite their being instructed to drink one liter of water per hour of rowing.

13. Victor Davis Hanson, *The Western Way of War* (New York: Alfred A. Knopf, 1989), 101–102. Nearly 25 percent of the American soldiers who responded to an anonymous survey during World War II admitted to having lost control of their bowels due to fear: Paul Fussell, "The Real War, 1939–1945," *Atlantic Monthly*, August 1989: http://www.theatlantic.com/past/docs/unbound/bookauth/battle/fussell.htm (last accessed 12/15/2012).

14. Physically demanding labor: Aristophanes, *Knights* 784–785, 1366–1368, *Wasps* 1118–1119. Sections of the oar crew could be rested, however, by having the oarsmen row in turns: Thucydides 3.49.3. Seat cushions: Thucydides 2.93.2. Side screens: Thucydides 7.40.5; Xenophon, *Hellenica* 1.6.19, 2.1.22.

15. Thranites' pay: Thucydides 6.31.3, with A. W. Gomme, A. Andrewes, and K. J. Dover, *A Historical Commentary on Thucydides*, vol. 4 (Oxford: Clarendon Press, 1970):

293–295. Team leaders: Morrison et al., *Athenian Trireme*, 236, 253–254; Boris Rankov, "Rowing Olympias: A Matter of Skill," in Shaw, *The Trireme Project*, 52, 55.

16. "Fast-spreading chaos": Rankov, "Rowing Olympias," 51–52. Audible signal: Morrison et al., *Athenian Trireme*, 248–256; Rankov, "Rowing Olympias," 52–56.

17. Private boats: Pseudo-Xenophon, *The Constitution of the Athenians*, 1.19–20. Training: Aristophanes, *Acharnians* 554; Herodotus 6.12.1; Thucydides 1.142.9, 2.86.5, 7.51.2; Xenophon, *Hellenica* 6.2.27–32. It's likely that the oarsmen had regular positions within the ship. This would have made embarking and disembarking more orderly, and it would have allowed the rowers to get used to working with the same group of people around them: Morrison, *Athenian Trireme*, 236; Xenophon, *Oeconomicus* 8.8. Untrained crews: Thucydides 8.95.2.

18. Thucydides 7.36.4.

19. Some scholars maintain: E.g., A. J. Holladay, "Further Thoughts on Trireme Tactics," *Greece & Rome* 35 (1988): 149. Oar-breaking: Diodorus 11.18.6, 13.99.3; Polybius 1.51.9, 16.4.14; Livy 36.44.6, 37.24.2. Polybius at 16.4.14 mentions shearing off the oars in conjunction with a *diekplous*, but the passage does not imply that it was an inevitable part of the *diekplous*.

20. E.g., J. F. Lazenby, "The Diekplous," *Greece & Rome* 34 (1987): 170.

21. Stationed behind the gaps: Donald Kagan, *The Fall of the Athenian Empire* (Ithaca: Cornell University Press, 1987): 345n67. *Kuklos*: Thucydides 2.83–84, 3.78.2; Herodotus 8.11.1.

22. Thucydides 2.84.1. Not a technical use of the term: Ian Whitehead, "The Periplous," *Greece & Rome* 34 (1987): 179–180. Not adopted in response to a *kuklos*: At 7.36.3–4, e.g., Thucydides writes that the Syracusans were confident about going into battle against the Athenians in their harbor. For one thing, the Syracusans' prows were stronger than the Athenians'. That was because the Athenians didn't attack prow to prow, but "after a *periplous* they used their rams." In the upcoming battle, meanwhile, while the Syracusans would prevent the Athenians from using their *diekplous*, "want of room would prevent them from performing the *periplous*." I suppose one would need room to sail around a *kuklos*, but above all one needed the enemy to assume that formation—which the Syracusans in their confidence surely had no intention of doing. To me it doesn't sound as if Thucydides had a *kuklos* in mind at all when writing this passage. Similarly, Xenophon, *Hellenica* 1.6.31, suggests that a *periplous* could be performed against an enemy in line abreast.

23. Thucydides 8.104.4.

24. H. T. Wallinga, *The Boarding-Bridge of the Romans* (Groningen: J. B. Wolters, 1956), 34n1, and "The Trireme and History," *Mnemosyne* 43 (1990): 145.

25. Whitehead, "Periplous," 178–185. Thucydides 2.91.3. Polybius, writing in the second century BC about a third-century battle, describes a similar action at 1.51.6.

26. Half a knot faster: Robin Oldfield, "Collision Damage in Triremes," in *The Final Report*, ed. Boris Rankov (Oxford: Oxbow Books, 2012), 223–224; J. T. Shaw, "Steering to Ram: The Diekplous and Periplous," in Shaw, *The Trireme Project*, 99–101.

27. Thucydides 2.89.8, cf. 2.83.2, 7.36.4.

28. Old-fashioned fighting: Thucydides 1.49.1–3. Syracusans' reinforced prows: Thucydides 7.36.2. Narrowest area ever: Thucydides 7.70.4. Final naval battle at Syracuse: Thucydides 7.60–71.

29. Emergency evacuation: Morrison et al., *Athenian Trireme*, 236–237. Corinthians at Corcyra: Thucydides 1.50.1.

30. Swimming: Herodotus 8.89; Plato, *Laws* 689d; Xenophon, *Hellenica* 1.6.17. Butchered by the enemy: Herodotus 8.76.2.

CHAPTER III: THE BATTLE OF ARGINUSAE: FROM MANNING THE FLEET TO COLLECTING CORPSES

1. Xenophon, *Hellenica* 1.6.24–25; Diodorus 13.97.1–2; cf. Plato, *Menexenus* 243c. Preparing a fleet for some time: A fragmentary inscription tentatively dated to 407 may be evidence of just such a building program. It appears to refer to shipwrights being dispatched to Macedon to build ships and send them from there to Athens: *Archaic Times to the End of the Peloponnesian War: Translated Documents of Greece and Rome*, ed. and trans. Charles W. Fornara (Baltimore: Johns Hopkins University Press, 1977), no. 161; Russell Meiggs and David Lewis, *A Selection of Greek Historical Inscriptions to the End of the Fifth Century B.C.*, rev. ed. (Oxford: Clarendon Press, 1969), no. 91. The Athenians may have paid for their new fleet by minting gold obtained by melting down statues of Nike and other treasures on the Acropolis: scholia to Aristophanes, *Frogs* 720.

2. Xenophon, *Hellenica* 1.6.24. Either assignment unusual: *Hippeis* could be called up for service as hoplites, but this was not standard practice (Lysias 14.10). Thucydides explicitly says at 3.16.1 that the *hippeis* were not required to serve with the fleet in 428, but the proper interpretation of the passage is not as clear as it might be: Glenn Richard Bugh, *The Horsemen of Athens* (Princeton: Princeton University Press, 1988), 106–107n76.

3. Masters and slaves serving together: Thucydides 7.13.2, with A. J. Graham, "Thucydides 7.13.2 and the Crews of Athenian Triremes," *Transactions and Proceedings of the American Philological Society* 122 (1992): 257–263. Aristophanes, *Frogs* 693–694: Cf. *Frogs* 33–34, with scholia, and 191. Destruction of Plataea: Thucydides 3.68.1–3. Plataean citizenship: Demosthenes 59.104.

4. Diodorus 13.97.1. Metics obliged to serve: David Whitehead, *The Ideology of the Athenian Metic* (Cambridge: Cambridge Philological Society, 1977), 154.

5. One hundred twenty ships: Xenophon, *Hellenica* 1.6.26. Diodorus says at 13.97.3 that Callicratidas took 140 ships. Waiting a bad idea: Donald Kagan, *Fall of the Athenian Empire* (Ithaca: Cornell University Press, 1987), 349–350.

6. Battle formations: Xenophon, *Hellenica* 1.6.29–31.

7. Xenophon, *Hellenica* 1.6.29. Xenophon doesn't say how many allied ships there were, but there must have been at least 7, as that would bring our total up to 150 vessels. *Epi de tautais* meaning "in addition to these": Kagan, *Fall of the Athenian Empire*, 345–346n9. Less natural interpretation: *Xenophon* Hellenika *I-II.3.10*, ed. and trans. Peter Krentz (Warminster, UK: Aris & Philips, 1989), 153–154.

8. Battle formations: Diodorus 13.98.3–4, 13.99.4. Battles in the harbor: Diodorus 13.77.5–13.79.6. V. J. Gray, "The Value of Diodorus Siculus for the Years 411–386 BC," *Hermes* 115 (1987): 85.

9. Genuine interruption in line: E.g., Krentz, *Xenophon* Hellenika, 154. Center posted in front of island: E.g., Kagan, *Fall of the Athenian Empire*, 345.

10. Frontage of twenty yards per ship: Kagan, *Fall of the Athenian Empire*, 342–344n59; H. T. Wallinga, "The Trireme and History," *Mnemosyne* 43 (1990): 142–143. Forty-five yards of frontage per ship: Godfrey Hutchinson, *Attrition: Aspects of Command in the*

Peloponnesian War (Stroud, UK: Spellmount, 2006), 201. The island is 1300 yards long north to south. The ships south of the island could have been posted at an angle to it such that less than 1300 yards of the island was interjected in the battle line. If so, my numbers for the length of the Athenian line would have to be adjusted downward, but my main point is the same: posting the Athenian center to the south of the island would result in the longest possible array.

11. Xenophon, *Hellenica* 1.6.29.

12. Protect from the *diekplous*: Xenophon, *Hellenica* 1.6.31. Too shallow to be navigable: At their shallowest the channels are 0.9 meters deep, and that measurement has been consistent for the last two hundred years, since records were first kept: Hutchinson, *Attrition*, xxxvi, 200–201. The draft of the reconstructed trireme *Olympias* is a bit more than a meter: J. S. Morrison, J. F. Coates, and N. B. Rankov, *The Athenian Trireme: The History and Reconstruction of an Ancient Greek Warship*, 2nd ed. (Cambridge: Cambridge University Press, 2000), 198 fig. 56.

13. 4900 yards: 1350 yards per wing (thirty ships x 45 yards) plus the Athenian center (900 yards), plus the length of the island (1300 yards). Prepared to perform the *diekplous* and the *periplous*: Xenophon, *Hellenica* 1.6.31.

14. Diodorus 13.99.3–5; Xenophon, *Hellenica* 1.6.33.

15. Xenophon, *Hellenica* 1.6.33–34; Diodorus 13.99–100. Spartan (at least seventy) and Athenian (twenty-five) ships lost: Xenophon, *Hellenica* 1.6.34, 1.7.25; Diodorus 13.100.3. Xenophon contradicts this information at 1.7.30, at least ostensibly, while relating a speech delivered in Athens probably in late October of 406. The speaker, Euryptolemus, says of the Athenians' rescue operations, "All together there were forty-seven [rescue ships], four for each of the twelve ships that were lost." Various attempts have been made to reconcile the numbers (e.g., Kagan, *Fall of the Athenian Empire*, 355; Krentz, *Xenophon* Hellenika, 168), but the passage remains perplexing.

16. Without suffering significant losses: Xenophon, *Hellenica* 1.7.30. The ships of the navarchs, taxiarchs, and Samians were sound after the battle, but we don't know what became of the seven or more allied ships that had been in the Athenian center. Hutchinson, *Attrition*, 202–203.

17. Diodorus (13.100.1) says that the Athenians pursued the Spartans *eph' ikanon*, which means something like "for an adequate distance." Unfortunately, this doesn't help us much in terms of pinpointing the length of the Athenians' pursuit. But if they chased the Spartans for about a half hour, rowing fast at nine knots, they would have covered four and a half nautical miles. A half hour of fast rowing—followed by at least as much time spent on the (probably slower) return trip—strikes me as "sufficient" under the circumstances, if not more than sufficient: the crews would already have been exhausted by this time from their exertions during the battle itself, and they had other matters to attend to.

18. Diodorus 13.100.4.

19. Recovering corpses not always possible: In their funeral procession for those who died during the first year of the war with Sparta, the Athenians included an empty bier to represent those whose bodies had not been recovered: Thucydides 2.34.3. Importance of a proper burial: The plot of Sophocles' play *Antigone* attests to this attitude, hinging as it does on the title character's fateful decision to bury her brother despite his having been forbidden burial as an enemy of the state. Cf. Plutarch, *Nicias* 6. "Throw earth upon it": Aelian, *Varia Historia* 5.14.

20. Rammed near Garipadasi: All the ships on the Athenian right wing had begun the battle, at least, within a mile of land. Estimates for the number of survivors: George Busolt, *Griechische Geschichte*, vol. 3, pt. 2 (Gotha: Friedrich Andreas Perthes, 1904), 1596: 2000 survivors; George Grote, *History of Greece*, vol. 8 (New York: Peter Fenelon Collier & Son, 1900), 186: "more than a thousand," but in note 1 he suggests that the number is 2500; Ludwig Herbst, *Die Schlacht bei den Arginusen* (Hamburg: J. A. Meissner, 1855), 37n51: 2000; Kagan, *Fall of the Athenian Empire*, 355 and n4: "well over a thousand."

21. Regrouping after battle: Grote, *History of Greece*, vol. 8, 190. One hundred twenty-five ships: This is not counting the thirty-eight ships still trapped in Mytilene. Debate at Arginusae: Xenophon, *Hellenica* 1.6.35, 1.7.5, 1.7.29–30; Diodorus 13.100.1.

22. "Wind and a great storm": Xenophon, *Hellenica* 1.6.35; Diodorus 13.100.2–3. Trophies: Herodotus 8.121; Thucydides 2.84.4. "Size of the waves": Diodorus 13.100.2. "Against the most desperate risks": Grote, *History of Greece*, vol. 8, 188–189. Patch of bad weather: Xenophon, *Hellenica* 1.6.28.

23. Xenophon, *Hellenica* 1.6.36–38; Diodorus 13.100.5–6.

24. Corpses left unburied: Diodorus 13.101.1, 13.101.2, 13.101.6; cf. Plato, *Menexenus* 243c. Failure to rescue survivors: Xenophon, *Hellenica* 1.7.4, 1.7.5, 1.7.6, 1.7.9, 1.7.11, 1.7.17, 1.7.31.

25. Battle of Sybota: Thucydides 1.54.1. Artemisium: Herodotus 8.12.1.

26. Guy on a barley tub: Xenophon, *Hellenica* 1.7.11. General in need of rescue: Xenophon, *Hellenica* 1.7.32; *Athenaion Politeia* 34.1. According to Diodorus (13.99.3), Callicratidas damaged the general Lysias's ship, so perhaps he was the general who needed saving. If the general was rescued before the storm, it would explain why he could be considered culpable and liable to the same punishment as his colleagues: he would have been rescued in time to take part in the deliberations at Arginusae after the battle.

CHAPTER IV: THE ATHENIANS AND THEIR GENERALS: DEMOCRACY AND ACCOUNTABILITY

1. "Feared the wrath of the people": Diodorus 13.101.5.

2. Cleisthenes' reforms: *Athenaion Politeia* 21; Herodotus 5.69. Tribal regiments: *Athenaion Politeia* 61.3; Thucydides 6.98.4; Xenophon, *Hellenica* 4.2.19.

3. Boule: *Athenaion Politeia* 43.2–49, 62.3. Ten months: The Athenians' political year was divided into ten months, but they also used a twelve-month lunar calendar, which determined the celebration of festivals. Since the lunar and solar calendars don't match up—a twelve-month lunar year is about eleven days shorter than a solar year—the Athenians had to insert extra (intercalary) months and days periodically to keep the two running in sync. (We likewise insert an intercalary day—February 29th, or "leap day"—into our calendars every four years [with some exceptions] so that our seasons remain consistent with the calendar.)

4. On the Athenian magistrates other than the councilors, see *Athenaion Politeia* 24.3, 50–62.

5. Xenophon, *Memorabilia* 1.2.9.

6. Election of generals: *Athenaion Politeia* 44.4; Pseudo-Xenophon, *The Constitution of the Athenians*, 1.3. Size of the Pnyx: In the fifth century, the part of the Pnyx where the rocky surface had been smoothed out had an area of about 2400 square meters, or 4.3 square feet per person, assuming an attendance of 6000. It was possible, however, for the crowd to overflow onto the rockier parts of the hill (Mogens Herman Hansen, *The*

Athenian Democracy in the Age of Demosthenes [Oxford: Blackwell, 1991], 128–132). Low-tech: See *Athenaion Politeia* 63–65 for the allotment machine (*kleroterion*) the Athenians devised for selecting jury panels, a device that Julian Dibbell has wonderfully described as possessing "a kind of Flintstonian majesty" (Dibbell, "Info Tech of Ancient Democracy," http://www.alamut.com/subj/artiface/deadMedia/agoraMuseum.html (last accessed 3/10/2013.) Voting by show of hands: Mogens Hansen, "How Did the Athenian *Ecclesia* Vote?," in *The Athenian Ecclesia I. A Collection of Articles, 1976–1983* (Copenhagen: Museum Tusculanum Press, 1983), 103–121.

7. Those who are known to have served previously are: Aristocrates, in 413, 410, 407; Diomedon, 412; Pericles, 409, 407; Thrasyllus, 411, 410, 409, 408. Conon had also served before, in 411, 407, and perhaps 414.

8. Thucydides 1.45.3, 6.8.2.

9. E.g., Thucydides 2.85.4, 7.8.1–2.

10. *Athenaion Politeia* 48.3, 61.2. The deposition of the general Timotheus in 373/2 is the first known use of the *apocheirotonia* ([Demosthenes] 49.10). Deposition of Pericles: Diodorus 12.45.4; Plutarch, *Pericles* 35; cf. Thucydides 2.65.3.

11. *Athenaion Politeia* 54.2.

12. Conon prosecutes Adeimantus: Demosthenes 19.191. Apollodorus prosecutes Autocles, Menon, and Timomachus: Mogens Herman Hansen, *Eisangelia: The Sovereignty of the People's Court in Athens in the Fourth Century B.C. and the Impeachment of Generals and Politicians*. (Odense: University Press of Southern Denmark, 1975), nos. 90, 91, and 95.

13. For the listed trials, see Debra Hamel, *Athenian Generals: Military Authority in the Classical Period* (Leiden: Brill, 1998), 141–146, nos. 4, 8, 9, 12, 13, 14, 15, 20, and 21. See also 136 fig. 1. There is weaker evidence that other generals were prosecuted (nos. 5, 6, 7, 10, 11, 17) or at least deposed (nos. 18, 19, and maybe 22) between 431 and 406.

14. Thucydides' exile: Thucydides 5.26.5. Fifteen talents: Plutarch, *Pericles* 35. A talent was a unit of weight, equal to about fifty-seven pounds, and the corresponding value of that weight of precious metals. Phormio: Scholia to Aristophanes, *Peace* 347.

15. Thucydides 1.49.

16. Thucydides 3.98.3–5, 3.102.3–4, 3.105–3.114.1.

17. Thucydides 7.42–47, 7.48.4.

18. Anytus acquitted: Hansen, *Eisangelia*, 84 no. 65. Before you celebrate Anytus's acquittal, you should know that ten years later, in 399, he was one of three men who prosecuted the philosopher Socrates (Plato, *Apology* 18b). Socrates was convicted in the trial and sentenced to death. Prevented from rounding Malea by storms: Diodorus 13.64.6. Winds at Cape Malea: Donald Engels, *Roman Corinth* (Chicago: University of Chicago Press, 1990), 51 and 159, table 6. Literary evidence for Malea: Herodotus 4.179.2; Homer, *Odyssey* 3.288, 4.514, 9.80; Strabo 8.6.20. "Help me Christ": Lionel Casson, *The Ancient Mariners: Seafarers and Sea Fighters of the Mediterranean in Ancient Times*, 2nd ed. (Princeton: Princeton University Press, 1991), 142. Corcyraeans: Herodotus 7.168.4.

19. *Athenaion Politeia* 27.5; Diodorus 13.64.6.

CHAPTER V: THE AFTERMATH IN ATHENS: TRIBUNALS AND TRIBULATIONS

1. Date of the battle: We know the battle of Arginusae was fought in 406/5 (Athenaeus 5.218a; Diodorus 13.99–100), but we don't know its precise date. According to Hellanicus,

news of the blockade reached Athens before the new year: he has the Athenians responding to the crisis by granting freedom to slaves in 407/6 (scholia to Aristophanes, *Frogs* 694). Diodorus, however, says the Athenians enrolled metics for service in 406/5 (13.97). If both are correct, the thirty days the Athenians spent preparing a fleet (Xenophon, *Hellenica* 1.6.24) must have straddled the new year. The first day of 406/5 was our June 29. (The Athenian year began with the first new moon after the summer solstice. In 406 B.C. that would have been June 29. See Nasa's catalogue of moon phases at http://eclipse.gsfc.nasa.gov/phase/phases-0499.html for the year -405—last accessed 5/15/2013.) If the Athenians spent about fifteen days after that preparing their fleet and perhaps another week sailing around collecting allies (Xenophon, *Hellenica* 1.6.25), that would give us a battle date around July 21. Since I may have underestimated times above, however, I would suggest the battle took place between late July and early August. Date of the generals' deposition: The proceedings against the generals were already under way in October (see chap. 5, note 16). Before then we need time for the news of the battle to reach Athens and for the Athenians to depose their generals, for the news of the deposition to travel to Samos and for the generals to sail home, and finally for Erasinides' fining and prosecution by Archedemus and the first meetings of the boule and assembly—four days of proceedings, interspersed by some number of days in which there was no related activity. If we give the whole business four or five weeks together, that gives us a deposition date of early to mid-September.

2. Letter to the demos and boule: Xenophon, *Hellenica* 1.7.4. Diodorus does not explicitly mention this letter, but some kind of communication between the generals and the government is implied at 13.101.1: "When the Athenians learned about the victory at Arginusae . . ." Vessels identified by name: A list of known trireme names, translated into English, is available online on The Classics Pages (http://www.users.globalnet.co.uk/~loxias/triremenames2.htm—last accessed 4/12/2013). (The site is written by Andrew Wilson, the author of Ἅρειος Ποτὴρ καὶ ἡ τοῦ φιλοσόφου λίθος, an Ancient Greek translation of J. K. Rowling's *Harry Potter and the Philosopher's Stone*.) Detail left out of report: Xenophon, *Hellenica* 1.7.17.

3. Precluded individual cremations: When circumstances permitted, the dead would be cremated individually, but in the event of a high number of fatalities, burning bodies singly and storing the remains separately would have been an impossible task. Mass cremations were likely common. Eighty-eight live oarsmen: The average Greek male of the day weighed about 148 pounds: J. S. Morrison, J. F. Coates, and N. B. Rankov, *The Athenian Trireme: The History and Reconstruction of an Ancient Greek Warship*, 2nd ed. (Cambridge: Cambridge University Press, 2000), 266. Modern cremations yield remains weighing about 3.5% of the body's original weight: http://www.ncbi.nlm.nih.gov/pubmed/9144931 (last accessed 4/12/2013). Just over 1,600 gallons: Basically, one pound of corpse will yield one cubic inch or one-tenth of a cup of remains. The handy Cremation Urn Size Calculator at http://www.mainelyurns.com/what-size-cremation-urn.html can do the math for you (last accessed 4/12/2013).

4. Diodorus 13.101.2. Donald Kagan, *The Fall of the Athenian Empire* (Ithaca: Cornell University Press, 1987), 363.

5. Diodorus 13.101.1–2.

6. Diodorus 13.101.2.

7. As has been suggested: Kagan, *Fall of the Athenian Empire*, 364. Resolved to depose them: Diodorus 13.101.4–5; Xenophon, *Hellenica* 1.7.1.

8. Xenophon divides his account of the trial and its aftermath into different stages by inserting various temporal expressions into his narrative. "After this" (*meta tauta* or *meta de tauta*): 1.7.3, 1.7.4, 1.7.5, 1.7.8, 1.7.16, 1.7.34; "then" (*enteuthen*): 1.7.9; "not much later" and "later" (*ou pollo chrono husteron* and *husteron*): both at 1.7.35. These transitions, however, don't always signify a jump in time or a change in venue.

9. Xenophon, *Hellenica* 1.7.2. After he contested his fine: Martin Ostwald, *From Popular Sovereignty to the Sovereignty of Law: Law, Society, and Politics in Fifth-Century Athens* (Berkeley: University of California Press, 1986), 436. Xenophon, however, does not signal a division with a temporal expression here (cf. note 8, above). Imprisonment in Athens: Danielle Allen, "Imprisonment in Classical Athens," *Classical Quarterly* 47 (1997): 121–135. Imprisoned as debtor: Douglas M. MacDowell, *The Law in Classical Athens* (Ithaca: Cornell University Press, 1978), 187.

10. "Uniquely guilty": Kagan, *Fall of the Athenian Empire*, 366; see also, e.g., A. Andrewes, "The Arginousai Trial," *Phoenix* 28 (1974): 113 and n4. "Tops at villainy": Aristophanes, *Frogs* 421, cf. 588.

11. Xenophon, *Hellenica* 1.7.3.

12. Xenophon, *Hellenica* 1.7.4, with Peter Krentz, *Xenophon* Hellenika *I–II.3.10* (Warminster: Aris & Philips, 1989), 160. As others have pointed out: E.g., Andrewes, "Arginousai Trial," 113, 118, 120. That the letters were sent is also consistent with what Xenophon (2.3.35) later has Theramenes say of his involvement in the Arginusae business: he wasn't the one who started it; the generals accused him first.

13. Xenophon, *Hellenica* 1.7.5–6.

14. Xenophon, *Hellenica* 1.7.7. Diodorus claims (13.101.5) that the generals returned to Athens with most of their men specifically to be of help in the trial.

15. Evidence of illegality: E.g., Bodil Due, "The Trial of the Generals in Xenophon's *Hellenica*," *Classica et Medievalia* 34 (1983): 36. "Speech was not permitted them": Xenophon, *Hellenica* 1.7.5. Nothing illegal had taken place: Ostwald, *Popular Sovereignty*, 438–439.

16. Mid-October: The intervention of the Apaturia between the assembly and the second meeting of the boule gives us our only indication of when in 406/5 the proceedings against the generals took place. We know that the Apaturia was celebrated on three consecutive days sometime during Pyanepsion, the fourth month in the Athenian lunar year (as opposed to the ten-month political year: see chap. 4, note 3). It probably fell between the fifteenth and twenty-ninth of that month (S. D. Lambert, *The Phratries of Attica* [Ann Arbor: University of Michigan Press, 1993], 157n80). In 406 B.C. the first day of Pyanepsion would have fallen on our September 25 (see chap. 5, note 1). The first day of the Apaturia, then, was celebrated sometime between October 9 (the fifteenth day of Pyanepsion) and October 23 (the twenty-ninth day). The meeting of the boule that followed could have taken place no earlier than October 12 and presumably not much later than October 23. Boule not called during festival days: Mogens Herman Hansen, *The Athenian Democracy in the Age of Demosthenes* (Oxford: Blackwell, 1991), 250–251. A hundred or more phratries: Lambert, *Phratries*, 19–20: between 30 and 140 phratries; Hansen, *Athenian Democracy*, 46: at least a hundred and possibly several hundred. Registration of sons in phratry: Lambert, *Phratries*, 143–189.

17. Xenophon, *Hellenica* 1.7.8. Diodorus 13.101.6. Role of Theramenes not mentioned: Lysias 12.36, 12.62–78; Xenophon, *Hellenica* 2.3.30–32. Riling Athenians not in Theramenes' interest: E.g., Krentz, *Xenophon* Hellenika, 162.

18. Xenophon, *Hellenica* 1.7.8–10.

19. Xenophon, *Hellenica* 1.7.11. George Grote, *History of Greece*, vol. 8 (New York: Peter Fenelon Collier & Son, 1900), 199n1.

20. Xenophon, *Hellenica* 1.7.12, 1.7.16, with Edwin Carawan, "The Trial of the Arginousai Generals and the Dawn of 'Judicial Review,'" *Dike* 10 (2007): 37–38, 43–53. It was not usual, but there was precedent for condemning groups by a single vote: Plutarch, *Moralia* 833e-834a; Lycurgus 1.113–114; Antiphon 5.69–70; cf. Aristophanes, *Lysistrata* 268–270. Xenophon (*Memorabilia* 1.1.18) and Plato (*Apology* 32b) both write, however, that judging the generals by a single vote was a transgression of *nomoi*.

21. *Graphe paranomon*: Hansen, *Athenian Democracy*, 205–212. "Whatever it wanted": Xenophon, *Hellenica* 1.7.12–13. Diodorus (13.101.6) goes further than Xenophon, claiming that the Athenians shouted down anyone who tried to speak in the generals' defense. But this clearly isn't true, given Euryptolemus's speech (Xenophon, *Hellenica* 1.7.16–34). At 13.102.5 Diodorus also writes that the Athenians were "out of their minds" (*parephronese*) when they sentenced the generals.

22. Disruptive speech: Dustin Gish, "Defending *Dēmokratia*: Athenian Justice and the Trial of the Arginusae Generals," in *Xenophon: Ethical Principles and Historical Enquiry*, ed. Fiona Hobden and Christopher Tuplin, 161–212 (Leiden: Brill Academic Publishers, 2012), 187–191, 196; Joseph Roisman, "Speaker-Audience Interaction in Athens: A Power Struggle," in *Free Speech in Classical Antiquity*, ed. Ineke Sluiter and Ralph M. Rosen (Leiden: Brill Academic Publishers, 2004), 264–268; Judith Tacon, "'Thorubos': Interventions, Interruptions, and Popular Involvement in the Athenian Assembly," *Greece & Rome* 48 (2001): 173–192. "People's will *was* the law": Mark Munn, *The School of History: Athens in the Age of Socrates* (Berkeley: University of California Press, 2000), 186. It was their prerogative: Ostwald, *Popular Sovereignty*, 444.

23. Xenophon, *Hellenica* 1.7.14.

24. Never held office: Plato, *Apology* 32b. Socrates had, however, served in the military on at least three occasions (Plato, *Apology* 28e). Socrates as *epistates*: At *Hellenica* 1.7.15 Xenophon claims only that Socrates was one of the *prytaneis*, but at *Memorabilia* 1.1.18 and 4.4.2 he says Socrates was *epistates*. Other sources only mention Socrates serving as *prytanis*: Athenaeus 217f-218a; Plato, *Apology* 32b, *Gorgias* 473e-474a. "He would do nothing": Xenophon, *Hellenica* 1.7.14–15.

25. Euryptolemus's speech: Xenophon, *Hellenica* 1.7.16–34. Defendants tried under the decree of Canonnus had to plead their cases before the demos while bound. If convicted they were executed by being thrown into a pit, the *barathron* (1.7.20–21). Xenophon does not mention the death penalty in connection with the second law he mentions, but that it forbade the defendant's burial in Athens and imposed "the severest penalty" on him if found guilty (1.7.22) suggests that someone convicted under the law would be executed.

26. Xenophon, *Hellenica* 1.7.34. Demanded a recount: Hansen, "How Did the Athenian Ecclesia Vote?," in *The Athenian Ecclesia I. A Collection of Articles, 1976–1983* (Copenhagen: Museum Tusculanum Press, 1983), 133; Ostwald, *Popular Sovereignty*, 441–442n123.

27. Xenophon, *Hellenica* 1.7.9.

28. Diodorus 13.102.1–3.

29. Not much later: Xenophon, *Hellenica* 1.7.35. Tempting to identify fellow accused: Mabel L. Lang, "Theramenes and Arginousai," *Hermes* 120 (1992): 277.

30. "Fingers of blame": This is a loose translation of a quite wonderful word: Callixenus's wickedness, Diodorus writes (13.102.2), was *daktulodeiktoumenen*, a passive participle that means literally to be "pointed at with a finger." "Everyone hated him": Xenophon, *Hellenica* 1.7.35; Suda, s.v. *enauein* (epsilon 1136).

31. Theramenes' reputation: Aristophanes, *Frogs*, 534–541, 967–970; Xenophon, *Hellenica* 2.3.30–31. His execution: Xenophon, *Hellenica* 2.3.51–56.

32. Xenophon, *Hellenica* 1.7.4–6. See page 77.

33. Xenophon, *Hellenica* 1.7.8. See pages 79–80.

34. Kagan, *Fall of the Athenian Empire*, 370n57.

35. Theramenes was elected to the generalship in the following year, in the spring of 405. He was rejected at his *dokimasia*, however, the routine scrutiny of a newly elected candidate's qualifications for office, and thus did not serve: Lysias 13.10. Some scholars have supposed that Theramenes' rejection was related to his role in the Arginusae business, but see Gabriel Adeleye, "The Arginusae Affair and Theramenes' Rejection at the *Dokimasia* of 405/4 B.C," *Museum Africum* 6 (1977/78): 94–99, for a persuasive argument against that connection.

36. Xenophon, *Hellenica* 1.7.5.

Epilogue

1. Xenophon, *Hellenica* 2.1.21–2.2.4; Diodorus 13.105–107. For the number of prisoners taken, see Plutarch, *Lysander* 13, *Alcibiades* 37; Pausanias 9.32.9. The other eight ships that escaped were under the command of Conon, whose confinement in Mytilene had led directly to the Battle of Arginusae. Conon did not return to Athens after Aegospotami. Diodorus (13.106.6) writes that this was because he "feared the wrath of the people." Xenophon says it was because he knew the Athenian cause was lost (*Hellenica* 2.1.20). Both explanations are probably true. Conon went instead to Cyprus. Later he joined the Persians in fighting Sparta at sea. He would return to Athens finally in 394 after leading a joint Athenian and Persian fleet to victory against the Spartans at Cnidus.

2. Thucydides 5.26.1; Xenophon, *Hellenica*, 2.2.9–23; Diodorus 13.107.2–5.

3. "Infamy of injustice": Walter Raleigh, *The Works of Sir Walter Raleigh*, vol. 5, *The History of the World*, bks. 3–4 (Oxford: Oxford University Press, 1829), 185–186; cf. Diodorus 13.103.1–2. "Infinity of examples": Charles Rollin, *The Ancient History of the Egyptians, Carthaginians, Assyrians, Babylonians, Medes and Persians, Macedonians and Grecians* (Boston: Samuel Walker, 1823), 1: 501. "Monstrous assemblage": Rollin, *Ancient History*, 408. "Most fatal strokes of faction": William Mitford, *The History of Greece* (London: T. Cadell, 1838), 3: 448–449. "Recoiled with force": Jennifer Tolbert Roberts, *Athens on Trial: The Antidemocratic Tradition in Western Thought* (Princeton: Princeton University Press, 1994), 175–207 (the quoted text appears at 186).

4. Cited at Dustin Gish, "Defending *Dēmokratia*: Athenian Justice and the Trial of the Arginusae Generals," in *Xenophon: Ethical Principles and Historical Enquiry*, ed. Fiona Hobden and Christopher Tuplin (Leiden: Brill Academic Publishers, 2012), 162n4.

SUGGESTED FURTHER READING

This book's notes are used primarily for citing and discussing ancient sources. References to modern scholarship are minimal. My debt to previous work on the topics addressed here therefore goes far beyond what I have been able to acknowledge, as should be clear from the discussion below. What follows is a listing of the principal secondary sources I consulted while preparing this volume. It is intended to serve as a guide for further inquiry into the battle at Arginusae and the ships and states that collided there in 406 B.C.

A good place to begin learning about fifth-century Greek history and the Peloponnesian War in particular is Donald Kagan's one-volume history of the period, *The Peloponnesian War* (New York: Viking, 2003). This can be supplemented by the same author's four-volume history (all published by Cornell University Press), which tells the story in greater detail, with a particular focus on political issues and including handy and profuse references to primary and secondary sources: *The Outbreak of the Peloponnesian War* (1969), *The Archidamian War* (1974), *The Peace of Nicias and the Sicilian Expedition* (1981), and *The Fall of the Athenian Empire* (1987). Victor Hanson offers a thematic approach to the Peloponnesian War in *A War Like No Other: How the Athenians and Spartans Fought the Peloponnesian War* (New York: Random House, 2005), with chapters on sieges, disease, and naval warfare, for example. It is an excellent read, but because of its nonlinear approach is perhaps better for readers who are already familiar with the general timeline of the war. John Lazenby's *The Peloponnesian War: A Military Study* (London: Routledge, 2004), which is more serious in tone than the above, is a commendably careful piece of scholarship.

J. E. Lendon covers the first ten years of the war in his *Song of Wrath: The Peloponnesian War Begins* (New York: Basic Books, 2010), a rousing read, packed with delicious bits of information, which focuses on the roles of honor and rank in the conflict. For an overview of fifth-century Greek history that's focused on Athens' fleet, see John Hale's *Lords of the Sea: The Triumph and Tragedy of*

Ancient Athens (New York: Viking, 2009). Other volumes consulted include George Grote, *History of Greece*, vol. 8 (New York: Peter Fenelon Collier & Son, 1900); Simon Hornblower, *The Greek World, 479–323 BC* (New York: Routledge, 2011); Godfrey Hutchinson, *Attrition: Aspects of Command in the Peloponnesian War* (Stroud, UK: Spellmount, 2006); Russell Meiggs, *The Athenian Empire* (Oxford: Clarendon Press, 1972); and Raphael Sealey, *A History of the Greek City States, ca. 700–338 B.C.* (Berkeley: University of California Press, 1976). For the Persian Wars, I find J. F. Lazenby, *The Defence of Greece, 490–479 BC* (Warminster, UK: Aris & Phillips, 1993) especially helpful. Barry Strauss's *The Battle of Salamis* (New York: Simon & Schuster, 2004), meanwhile, is a very readable account of that important battle.

For an introduction to the Spartans, see Paul Cartledge, *The Spartans: The World of the Warrior-Heroes of Ancient Greece* (New York: Vintage Books, 2003), and J. F. Lazenby, *The Spartan Army* (Mechanicsburg, PA: Stackpole Books, 2012). See also Cameron Hawkins "Spartans and *Perioikoi*: The Organization and Ideology of the Lakedaimonian Army in the Fourth Century," *Greek, Roman, and Byzantine Studies* 51 (2011): 401–434, and Brandon D. Ross, "*Krypteia*: A Form of Ancient Greek Warfare," *Grand Valley Journal of History* 1 (2011) (available at http://scholarworks.gvsu.edu/gvjh/vol1/iss2/4/). On the strategy of ravaging fields, which the Spartans adopted during their invasions of Attica, see especially Victor Davis Hanson, *Warfare and Agriculture in Classical Greece* (Berkeley: University of California Press, 1998).

Our principal sources for the fifth century are the historians Herodotus, Thucydides, and Xenophon. The Landmark translations of these texts, edited by Robert B. Strassler, are enormously helpful because of their numerous maps and the wealth of information to be found in their appendixes, including essays on the size of Xerxes' forces in 480, hoplite and trireme warfare, and the battle at Arginusae and its aftermath: *The Landmark Herodotus*, translated by Andrea L. Purvis (New York: Pantheon Books, 2007); *The Landmark Thucydides*, translated by Richard Crawley (New York: Free Press, 1996); *The Landmark Xenophon's* Hellenika, translated by John Marincola (New York: Pantheon Books, 2009).

I consulted the following commentaries while preparing this text: Kenneth Dover, *Aristophanes: Frogs*, (Oxford: Clarendon Press, 1993); A. W. Gomme, A. Andrewes, and K. J. Dover, *A Historical Commentary on Thucydides*, vols. 1–4 (Oxford: Oxford University Press, 1945–1981); Simon Hornblower, *A Commentary on Thucydides*, vols. 1–3 (Oxford: Clarendon Press, 1991–2009); *Xenophon* Hellenika *I-II.3.10*, ed. and trans. Peter Krentz (Warminster, UK: Aris & Philips,

1989); J. M. Moore, *Aristotle and Xenophon on Democracy and Oligarchy* (Berkeley: University of California Press, 1975); P. J. Rhodes, *A Commentary on the Aristotelian* Athenaion Politeia (Oxford: Clarendon Press, 1981); *Thucydides: History III*, ed. and trans. P. J. Rhodes (Warminster, UK: Aris & Phillips, 1994); G. E. Underhill, *A Commentary on the Hellenica of Xenophon* (Oxford: Clarendon Press, 1900).

On triremes in general and the modern trireme *Olympias* in particular, see especially J. S. Morrison, J. F. Coates, and N. B. Rankov, *The Athenian Trireme: The History and Reconstruction of an Ancient Greek Warship*, 2nd ed. (Cambridge: Cambridge University Press, 2000). Their discussion of the *Olympias* can be supplemented with *Building the Trireme* (London: Constable, 1988), by Frank Welsh, who offers a behind-the-scenes look at the project. See also the website of the Trireme Trust at http://www.triremetrust.org.uk. The results of the sea trials of the *Olympias* have been fully published in four volumes: J. S. Morrison and J. F. Coates, *An Athenian Trireme Reconstructed: The British Sea Trials of* Olympias (Oxford: British Archaeological Reports, 1989); J. F. Coates, S. K. Platis, and J. T. Shaw, *The Trireme Trials, 1988* (Oxford: Oxbow Books, 1990); Timothy Shaw, ed., *The Trireme Project: Operational Experience, 1987–90, Lessons Learnt* (Oxford: Oxbow Books, 1993); and Boris Rankov, ed., *The Final Report* (Oxford: Oxbow Books, 2012). Of especial interest are the following articles from those volumes: Robin Oldfield, "Collision Damage in Triremes," in Rankov, *Final Report*, 214–224; Boris Rankov, "Rowing Olympias: A Matter of Skill," and "Steering to Ram: The Diekplous and Periplous," in Shaw, *Trireme Project*, 50–57 and 99–104; Timothy Shaw, "Is Olympias a Trieres?," in Shaw, *Trireme Project*, 105–107; Andrew Taylor, "Battle Manoeuvres for Fast Triremes," and Ian Whitehead, "*Triereis* under Oar and Sail," in Rankov, *Final Report*, 231–243 and 155–160. For discussion of the validity of the design of the *Olympias* and proposed changes to it, see John Coates, "Tilley's and Morrison's Triremes—Evidence and Practicality," *Antiquity* 69 (1995): 159–162, and Alec Tilley, "Three Men to a Room—A Completely Different Trireme," *Antiquity* 66 (1992): 599–610. On triremes, see also J. G. Landels, *Engineering in the Ancient World*, 2nd ed. (Berkeley: University of California Press, 2000), and J. S. Morrison and R. T. Williams, *Greek Oared Ships, 900–322 B.C.* (Cambridge: Cambridge University Press, 1968).

The relevant chapters of Hans van Wees, *Greek Warfare: Myths and Realities* (London: Bristol Classical Press, 2004), and Victor Hanson, *A War Like No Other* (cited above), provide excellent introductions to ancient naval warfare. I also consulted Lionel Casson, *The Ancient Mariners: Seafarers and Sea Fighters of the*

Mediterranean in Ancient Times, 2nd ed. (Princeton: Princeton University Press, 1991), and "The Feeding of the Trireme Crews and an Entry in *IG* II^2 1631," *Transactions of the American Philological Association* 125 (1974): 261–269; A. W. Gomme, "A Forgotten Factor of Greek Naval Strategy," in *Essays in Greek History and Literature* (Oxford: Blackwell, 1937), 190–203; Cynthia M. Harrison, "Triremes at Rest: On the Beach or in the Water?," *Journal of Hellenic Studies* 119 (1999): 168–171; J. F. Lazenby, "Essays and Reflections: Naval Warfare in the Ancient World: Myths and Realities," *International History Review* 9 (1987): 438–455. On the organization of Athens' fleet, see Vincent Gabrielsen, *Financing the Athenian Fleet* (Baltimore: Johns Hopkins University Press, 1994), and Borimir Jordan, *The Athenian Navy in the Classical Period: A Study of Athenian Naval Administration and Military Organization in the Fifth and Fourth Centuries B.C.* (Berkeley: University of California Press, 1975).

For the battle tactics of oar-breaking, the *diekplous*, and the *periplous*, see A. J. Holladay, "Further Thoughts on Trireme Tactics," *Greece & Rome* 35 (1988): 149–151; J. F. Lazenby, "The Diekplous," *Greece & Rome* 34 (1987): 169–177; Thomas G. Papps, "The Mysterious 'Diekplous,'" *Naval History* 19.1 (2005): 35–38; J. T. Shaw, "Steering to Ram: The Diekplous and Periplous" (cited above); W. W. Tarn, *Hellenistic Military and Naval Developments* (Cambridge: Cambridge University Press, 1930); H. T. Wallinga, *The Boarding-Bridge of the Romans: Its Construction and Its Function in the Naval Tactics of the First Punic War* (Groningen: J. B. Wolters, 1956), and "The Trireme and History," *Mnemosyne* 43 (1990): 132–149; Ian Whitehead, "The Periplous," *Greece & Rome* 34 (1987): 178–185.

On deaths at sea, see Barry Strauss, "Perspectives on the Death of Fifth-Century Athenian Seamen," in *War and Violence in Ancient Greece*, edited by Hans van Wees (London: Classical Press of Wales, 2000), 261–284. On the cremation of Greek war dead, see W. Kendrick Pritchett, *The Greek State at War. Part 4* (Berkeley: University of California Press, 1985). And on the problem of identifying the dead (in this case infantry deaths, but anyone dealing with corpses after a naval battle would have faced comparable problems), see Pamela Vaughn, "The Identification and Retrieval of the Hoplite Battle-Dead," in *Hoplites: The Classical Greek Battle Experience*, edited by Victor Davis Hanson (London: Routledge, 1991), 38–62.

On the roll of slaves in Athens' navy, see M. Amit, *Athens and the Sea: A Study in Athenian Sea-Power* (Brussels: Latomus, 1965); Lionel Casson, "Galley Slaves," *Transactions and Proceedings of the American Philological Society* 97 (1966): 35–44; Yvon Garlan, *Slavery in Ancient Greece* (Ithaca, NY: Cornell University Press, 1982); A. J. Graham, "Thucydides 7.13.2 and the Crews of Athenian Triremes,"

Transactions and Proceedings of the American Philological Society 122 (1992): 257–270, and "Thucydides 7.13.2 and the Crews of Athenian Triremes: An Addendum," *Transactions of the American Philological Association* 128 (1998): 89–114; Peter Hunt, *Slaves, Warfare, and Ideology in the Greek Historians* (Cambridge: Cambridge University Press, 1998); Rachel L. Sargent, "The Use of Slaves by the Athenians in Warfare," *Classical Philology* 22 (1927): 264–279. For discussion of the grant of freedom offered to the slaves who enrolled for service in 406, see also Peter Hunt, "The Slaves and the Generals of Arginusae," *American Journal of Philology* 122 (2001): 359–380; Susan Lape, *Race and Citizen Identity in the Classical Athenian Democracy* (Cambridge: Cambridge University Press, 2010); Michael J. Osborne, *Naturalization in Athens*, vol. 3 (Brussels: Academie voor Wetenschappen, Letteren en Schone Kunsten, 1983); Ian Worthington, "Aristophanes' 'Frogs' and Arginusae," *Hermes* 117 (1989): 359–363. For related discussion, see Luca A. Asmonti, "The Arginusae Trial, the Changing Role of *Strategoi* and the Relationship between *Demos* and Military Leadership in Late-Fifth Century Athens," *Bulletin of the Institute of Classical Studies* 49 (2006): 1–21.

I argue in the narrative that the Athenian fleet was arranged in two lines abreast at Arginusae. J. S. Morrison, one of the triumvirate behind the construction of the modern trireme *Olympias*, holds the rather eccentric view that the ships were instead arranged in columns. See (in addition to *The Athenian Trireme* and *Greek Oared Ships*, cited above) J. S. Morrison, "Greek Naval Tactics in the 5th Century BC," *International Journal of Nautical Archaeology and Underwater Exploration* 3 (1974): 21–26, and "The Greek Ships at Salamis and the Diekplous," *Journal of Hellenic Studies* 111 (1991): 196–200. Against Morrison's view, see, e.g., J. K. Anderson, review of *Greek Oared Ships, 900–322 B.C.*, by J. S. Morrison and R. T. Williams, *Classical Philology* 64 (1969): 180–183, and J. F. Lazenby, Review of *The Athenian Trireme: The History and Reconstruction of an Ancient Greek Warship*, by J. S. Morrison and J. F. Coates, *Journal of Hellenic Studies* 108 (1988): 250.

Mogens Herman Hansen's *The Athenian Democracy in the Age of Demosthenes* (Oxford: Blackwell, 1991) is an indispensable guide to the workings of the Athenian state. It can also serve to point readers to relevant works in the author's vast corpus of publications. On the boule, see P. J. Rhodes, *The Athenian Boule* (Oxford: Clarendon Press, 1972). For legal matters, see also S. C. Todd, *The Shape of Athenian Law* (Oxford: Clarendon Press, 1993), and Douglas M. MacDowell, *The Law in Classical Athens* (Ithaca, NY: Cornell University Press, 1978). On Athens' magistrates, see Robert Develin, *Athenian Officials, 684–321 B.C.* (Cambridge: Cambridge University Press, 1989). For the generalship in particular, see Charles W. Fornara, *The Athenian Board of Generals from 501 to 404* (Wiesbaden: Franz Steiner Verlag, 1971); Debra Hamel, *Athenian Generals: Military Authority in the Classical Period* (Leiden: Brill, 1998); Jennifer Tolbert Roberts, *Accountability in Athenian Government* (Madison: University of Wisconsin Press, 1982).

The battle at Arginusae and its immediate aftermath are discussed in many of the more general histories cited elsewhere in this essay. For further discussion, see also Robert J. Buck, *Thrasybulus and the Athenian Democracy: The Life of an Athenian Statesman* (Stuttgart: Franz Steiner Verlag, 1998), and Graham Wylie, "The Battle of Arginusae: A Reappraisal," *Civiltà Classica e Cristiana* 11 (1990): 234–249.

For the trial against the generals, see A. Andrewes, "The Arginousai Trial," *Phoenix* 28 (1974): 112–122; Edwin Carawan, "The Trial of the Arginousai Generals and the Dawn of 'Judicial Review,'" *Dike* 10 (2007): 19–56; Paul Cloché, "L'Affaire des Arginuses (406 Avant J.-C.)," *Revue Historique* 130 (1919): 5–68; Bodil Due, "The Trial of the Generals in Xenophon's *Hellenica*," *Classica et Mediaevalia* 34 (1983): 33–44; Dustin Gish, "Defending *Dēmokratia*: Athenian Justice and the Trial of the Arginusae Generals," in *Xenophon: Ethical Principles and Historical Enquiry*, edited by Fiona Hobden and Christopher Tuplin (Leiden: Brill Academic Publishers, 2012), 161–212; Mabel L. Lang, "Illegal Execution in Ancient Athens," *Proceedings of the American Philosophical Society* 134 (1990): 24–29; B. M. Lavelle, "*Adikia*, the Decree of Kannonus, and the Trial of the Generals," *Classica et Mediaevalia* 39 (1988): 19–41; Martin Ostwald, *From Popular Sovereignty to the Sovereignty of Law* (Berkeley: University of California Press, 1986); Frances Pownall, "Shifting Viewpoints in Xenophon's *Hellenica*," *Athenaeum* 88 (2000): 499–513; Jennifer Tolbert Roberts, "Arginusae Once Again," *Classical World* 71 (1977): 107–111; Tim Rood, "The Arginusae Trial," in *Xenophon and His World*, edited by Christopher Tuplin (Wiesbaden: Franz Steiner Verlag, 2004), 374–395.

On the slippery statesman Theramenes, see Gabriel Adeleye, "The Arginusae Affair and Theramenes' Rejection at the *Dokimasia* of 405/4 B.C.," *Museum Africum* 6 (1977/78): 94–99; Robert J. Buck, "The Character of Theramenes," *Ancient History Bulletin* 9 (1995): 14–24; Mabel L. Lang, "Theramenes and Arginousai," *Hermes* 120 (1992): 267–279; B. Perrin, "The Rehabilitation of Theramenes," *American Historical Review* 9 (1904): 649–669.

Finally, for discussion of the hostility to Athens' democracy that was inspired in part by the Arginusae episode, see Dustin Gish, "In Defense of Democracy: Antidemocratic Sentiment and Democratic Deliberation from Ancient Athens to the American Founding," in *Democratic Decision-Making: Historical and Contemporary Perspectives*, edited by David Lewis Schaefer (Lanham, MD: Lexington Books, 2012), 57–82; Mogens Herman Hansen, "The Tradition of the Athenian Democracy, A.D. 1750–1990," *Greece & Rome* 39 (1992): 14–30; A. H. M. Jones, "The Athenian Democracy and Its Critics," *Cambridge Historical Journal* 11 (1953): 1–26; and especially Jennifer Tolbert Roberts, *Athens on Trial: The Antidemocratic Tradition in Western Thought* (Princeton: Princeton University Press, 1994).

INDEX

Page numbers in *italics* refer to figures.